THE ADVENT... ...LICE

Alice Liddell at the age Lewis Carroll always liked to remember her:
'an entirely fascinating little seven-year-old maiden'.

The Story of
ALICE

The story behind the stories
Lewis Carroll told

MAVIS BATEY

MACMILLAN
CHILDREN'S BOOKS

First published 1991 by Macmillan Children's Books,
a division of Macmillan Publishers Limited.
25 Eccleston Place, London SW1W 9NF,
and Basingstoke.

Associated companies worldwide.

ISBN 0 333 73879 9

1 3 5 7 9 8 6 4 2

A CIP catalogue record for this book is available
from the British Library.

Typeset by Macmillan Production Limited
Printed by Mackays of Chatham plc, Kent.

*For my granddaughter Rachel Alice
who also liked stories about herself*

Picture Acknowledgements

The Illustrated London News (p. 79); the Bodleian Library, Oxford (p. 75); Oxfordshire County Council, Department of Leisure and Arts (p. 85); National Portrait Gallery, London (p. 3); The British Library (p. 97); the Governing Body, Christ Church, Oxford (pp. 13, 31, 50 and 53); and Graham Ovenden (pp. ii and 26). The Tenniel illustrations are reproduced from prints taken from the original wood engravings (*Sir John Tenniel's illustrations to Lewis Carroll's Alice's Adventures in Wonderland* and *Through the Looking-Glass* – Macmillan, 1988)

Contents

I

'Tell us a Story'

Alice's Adventures in Wonderland, known and beloved by children and adults the world over, was first published, by Macmillan, over 125 years ago. The stories have a unique, fresh quality because they were told to a real child on the spur of the moment and have captured for all time the wonder of childhood and its 'happy summer days'. At the time of their telling there was no intention of publication. Lewis Carroll, a shy Oxford don whose real name was the Reverend Charles Dodgson, was one of the most gifted story-tellers of all time and a lover of children with a deep understanding of their minds and an appreciation of their points of view, qualities stemming from his own childhood experiences and happy summer days. All the magic moments of life, and its heartaches, were stored in his mind and, 'ever drifting down the stream' of life, he had instant recall of them. A young girl whom he befriended in his sixties could still say of him: 'The truth of the matter is that he had the heart of a child himself' (Cohen, 1989, p. 124).

Carroll knew that to capture a child's wholehearted attention in story-telling the child must remain at the centre of the story, in familiar surroundings, preferably those in which the tale was being told. From this safe foundation the story-teller could follow where the child's imagination suggested and lead it spell-bound into an unexpected Wonderland:

Anon, to sudden silence won,
In fancy they pursue
The dream-child moving through a land
Of wonders wild and new,
In friendly chat with bird or beast –
And half believe it true.

'At once he caught my idea and off he would go with a fresh series of adventures,' remembered one little girl (Cohen, 1989, p. 138). On another occasion a mother who listened to the stories about sea urchins and ammonites coming to life, told to her two open-mouthed young daughters at the seaside, exclaimed without hesitation, 'You must be the author of *Alice's Adventures.*' The story-teller laughed but looked astonished, and said, 'My dear Madam, my name is Dodgson, and *Alice's Adventures* was written by Lewis Carroll.' But the lady insisted, 'Then you must have borrowed the name, for only he could have told a story as you have just done' (Collingwood, 1898, p. 99).

The Wonderland stories told to the countless Beatrices, Gertrudes, Olives, Ediths and Ruths, although not written down, became the child's own prized possessions, treasured all the more in large Victorian families where everything had to be shared. Their stories are lost to us, but for Alice it was different: she was immortalised when she pestered Lewis Carroll to write down the stories that were told to her, stories he was later persuaded by friends to publish. The Alice books begin with the word 'Alice' and it is Alice who is the unmistakable heroine of the two volumes, present on every page, 'as large as life and twice as natural'.

Alice was Alice Liddell, the daughter of the Dean of Christ Church, Oxford, the college at which Charles Dodgson, a mathematician and logician, was a lecturer.

2

Charles Lutwidge Dodgson (1832–98), alias Lewis Carroll (derived from his mother's maiden name Lutwidge, the German for Lewis, and the Latin for Charles – Carolus), at the age of twenty-four, the year he met Alice.

'Tell us a story' was the constant cry of the Dean's three daughters whenever they met Mr Dodgson at his rooms or in their nursery and, as Alice herself has said, the stories grew into 'new tales owing to the frequent interruptions, which opened up fresh and undreamed-of possibilities'. Although Lewis Carroll had scores of child friends all through his life, there was something about Alice Liddell that stimulated his literary genius for nonsense and make-believe in a way that had never happened to him before and would never be repeated. 'Let's pretend' had always been Alice's favourite phrase, Lewis Carroll tells us, but although the worlds of *Wonderland* and *Looking-Glass* are fantasy, they too are based on Alice's own adventures with her don friend: walks round Oxford, trips on the Thames, a visit to her grandmother, local entertainments and games in her nursery or the Deanery garden. Alice said that people who were present at the time of the story-telling featured as characters in the fairy-tale, and we can recognise Alice's sisters, her governess, Carroll's brothers and sisters, and colleagues who accompanied them on the river excursions. Carroll's diaries, Alice's published recollections, colleagues' reminiscences, Oxford newspapers and college and university records enable us to piece together the real adventures behind the nonsense tales. In many ways how the stories came to be written is as fascinating as the stories themselves.

II

The Beginning of Wonderland

Wonderland, as a place where exciting stories are made out of everyday events, began at Lewis Carroll's birthplace, Daresbury in Cheshire, where his father, the Reverend Charles Dodgson, was the incumbent from 1827 until 1843. It was a poor living, and the parsonage where the future Lewis Carroll was born in 1832, the eldest son and third of eleven children, was so remote from the community that his nephew said a passing farm cart was an exciting event for the children. Charles's contribution to helping his over-worked mother run the household was entertaining his brothers and sisters. When they moved to Croft in 1843 the family consisted of Frances fifteen, Elizabeth thirteen, Charles eleven, Caroline ten, Mary eight, Skeffington seven, Wilfred five, Louisa three, and Henrietta a baby. Edwin was born three years after they had settled in. Croft provided a better living and a more spacious house and, being situated on the main road from York to Darlington by the bridge over the river Tees, gave Charles scope for more inventive stories and entertainment. Darlington was famous for the first passenger railway and Croft had its own station so, not surprisingly, the young Charles invented the Dodgson Railway Game, in the Rectory garden, by using a wheel-barrow and barrels as the train and building stations, booking offices and refreshment rooms. In spite of taking up most of the garden paths, his long-suffering mother

5

He was born at ✧ ✧
Daresbury Parsonage,
Jan. 27, 1832, and died
at Guildford, Jan. 14, 1898.

Lewis Carroll Memorial Window at All Saints, Daresbury, Cheshire,
where his father was the incumbent from 1827 to 1843.

seemed only too delighted to condone 'the Railroad games, which the darlings all delight in' (Cohen, 1989, p. 9). The whimsical rules of the game showed some of the more perverse traits of Wonderland adventures:

> All passengers when upset are requested to lie still until picked up – as it is requisite that at least 3 trains should go over them, to entitle them to the attention of the doctor and assistants.

Also, as a skit on *Bradshaw's Railway Guide*, Charles devised a ballad opera 'La Guida di Bragia' for the marionette theatre he had made with the assistance of members of the family.

At Croft Charles developed the conjuring and puzzle-making skills that were to delight young friends for the rest of his life. In 1950 a childish treasure trove was found hidden under a loose board in the nursery floor, which in addition to a thimble, a child's left shoe, the shell of a lobster and the lid from a doll's tea-set, revealed a wooden block inscribed by the future author of *Wonderland*:

> *And we'll wander through*
> *the wide world*
> *and chase the buffalo.*

Soon after his arrival at Croft he began to write down and illustrate whimsical sketches and poems in family magazines, the first of which was called *Useful and Instructive Poetry*. Already there appear the seeds for stories told later to Alice: a drawing of a very long dog's tail, a forerunner of the Mouse's tail, called 'A Tale of a Tail', and a poem about a boy who sat on a wall, but, like Humpty Dumpty, eventually fell off. The magazines were continued in vacations from his schools at Richmond, where he went in 1844, and Rugby three years later. In 1850 the family was brought closer together when Charles came home to study for Oxford entrance, and much of the magazine the *Rectory Umbrella*, called after the sheltering yew tree under which the children played in the Rectory garden, was written at this time. The mock scholarly footnotes reflect his introduction to university reading. The frontispiece showed an open umbrella marked Tales, Poetry, Fun, Riddles, Jokes dispelling demons of Gloom, Spite, Ennui, Alloverishness, Crossness and Woe, the fun all part of a worked out plan to meet life's vicissitudes with humour and fortitude.

One of the mock-heroic poems in the *Rectory Umbrella*, 'Lays of Sorrow No. 2', in which the young Carroll illustrates an outsize 'ancient Rectory' from which sally forth 'the children of the North', tells of the valour of the knight Ulfrid Longbow (his brother Wilfred Longley) keeping the road to Croft, aided by the fair Flureeza (his sister Louisa Fletcher). The last of the magazines of humorous stories and parodies was *Mischmasch*, collected for the family after Charles had started life as an Oxford undergraduate.

However, before he had even settled in at Christ Church he was recalled to Croft when his mother died early in 1851. Broken-hearted he returned to Oxford after the funeral and an aunt, Lucy Lutwidge, moved into the Rectory to care for the family, the youngest of whom was still under five. Charles returned to Croft every vacation until his father died in 1868, when he brought his sisters down south and set up house for them at the Chestnuts, Guildford. He felt responsible for his sisters, only one of whom married, throughout his life.

For Charles Dodgson, Christ Church had already become

much more than a place of work, and for forty-seven years it continued as a way of life. He arrived as an undergraduate in January 1851, at the age of nineteen, and remained there, except for vacations, for the rest of his life. He took a first-class degree in mathematics, was elected to a Studentship (the equivalent of a Fellowship in other colleges), was ordained deacon, became a member of the Governing Body, and for nine years was Curator of the Common Room. His main preoccupation was mathematics, and, but for Alice Liddell, his only published works might well have been those on algebra, geometry and logic. His lifelong friend, Professor Bartholomew Price (of 'Twinkle, twinkle little Bat' fame, see page 20), maintained that Carroll's achievement was unique, being founded on 'the unusual combination of deep mathematic ability and taste with the genius that led to the writing of *Alice's Adventures*' (Cohen, 1989, p. 261).

When the fairy-tales Carroll wrote for Alice Liddell became famous he shrank from the publicity the acknowledged authorship would have brought him. In later years letters addressed to Lewis Carroll, Christ Church, Oxford, were returned to the Post Office as 'not known', and the Bodleian Library received a sharp rebuke for a catalogue entry linking Charles Dodgson, the author of *An Elementary Treatise on Determinants*, with Lewis Carroll, the author of *Alice's Adventures in Wonderland*. Many people in Oxford knew his secret, of course, and eagerly awaited fresh masterpieces of nonsense. 'No, it is not funny – it's about Euclid,' was Carroll's firm reply to the hopeful enquiry of a lady who called on him one afternoon when he was engrossed in writing a new book. However, Lewis Carroll himself publicly denied the persistent rumour that Queen Victoria, having read *Alice* with pleasure, asked for the author's next book to be sent to her and was not amused when she received a geometry text book.

Although make-believe and mathematics had to be kept apart, there was no personality split between Dodgson the don and clergyman and Carroll the inventor of fairy-tales; his imaginative writing, logical mind, religious faith and love of children were all of a piece. A delight in make-believe may seem inconsistent with a logical mind, but his imaginative genius was a unique brand of fun-loving non-sense based on logic which appealed instantly to children, especially to an observant, enquiring child like Alice. We cannot tell when the special 'Alice' story-telling began as Carroll's diaries for April 1858 until May 1862 are missing, by which time we know the stories were in full swing.

It was not nonsense tales but his newly acquired camera that first brought Carroll into contact with Alice Liddell, shortly after the Dean's family had taken up residence at Christ Church. His diary entry for 25 April 1856, the year after the Dean's appointment, reads:

> Went over with [Reginald] Southey in the afternoon to the Deanery, to try and take a photograph of the Cathedral: both attempts proved failures. The three little girls were in the garden most of the time, and we became excellent friends: we tried to group them in the foreground of the picture, but they were not patient sitters. I mark this day with a white stone.

The 'white stone' in his diary was reserved for days which he thought would have particular significance in his life. Charles Dodgson could not have guessed that this day would mark the beginning of a child friendship which was to inspire one of the world's most famous books and bring him universal fame as Lewis Carroll.

III

Wonderland Schooling

Carroll continued to collate the *Mischmasch* stories for the family right up until 1862, the year that Alice fell down the rabbit-hole and changed the course of his life. A poem, 'She's all my fancy painted Him', from one of the later Croft family magazines actually appears as a filler in *Alice's Adventures in Wonderland*, with the omission of the first verse.

> *They told me you had been to her,*
> *And mentioned me to him:*
> *She gave me a good character*
> *But said I could not swim.*

The fairy-tales Lewis Carroll told to Alice were not always new ones, but came from the treasure trove of stories he had already told to children, either at home or on seaside holidays. These would be adapted to the situation and, of course, include a point of contact with Alice's own experiences. Such episodes include the stories about the Mock Turtle and the Gryphon and their discussion of the way schools are regulated in the sea.

The first recorded instance of Carroll extending his story-telling from the family to strangers was given by Thomas Fowler, who was with him on Professor Price's Oxford maths reading party at Whitby in 1854. In an obituary notice in 1898, Fowler, who was then President of Corpus

Christi College, recalled that it was there 'that *Alice* was incubated. Dodgson used to sit on a rock on the beach telling stories to a circle of eager young listeners of both sexes.' Fowler and Dodgson had remained good friends throughout their Oxford careers, frequently dining and going for walks together. On one occasion, in 1882, Fowler invited him to dine in hall with William Ranken, a fellow companion on Price's Whitby reading party, and Carroll recorded in his diary: 'Both men are now mostly bald, with quite grey hair: yet how short a time it seems, since we were both undergraduates together at Whitby in 1854!'

Thomas Fowler had not meant, of course, that the actual stories told to the fascinated Whitby children were to be found in *Alice*, for her adventures were, as we know, told on the spot. In later years Reverend Robinson Duckworth ('the Duck') described the famous 'voyage to Godstow' and recalled how he turned round in the boat and asked, 'Dodgson, is this an extempore romance of yours?' and received the answer, 'Yes, I'm inventing as we go along' (Cohen, 1989, p. 31). What Fowler had recognised when *Alice's Adventures in Wonderland* came to be published was the whimsical sense of humour and word-play which had delighted the children on the sands ten years before. It was probably the very same seaside fun of the school in the sea, where the master was an old Turtle called Tortoise because he 'taught us' and lessons 'lessened' every day until there had to be a day off, that had amused the future Professor of Logic and stuck in his mind.

The story of Alice's adventures with the Mock Turtle and the Gryphon, which included these drolleries, was told for a special reason, at a time when Carroll's brother Wilfred and possibly Skeffington, both undergraduates at Christ Church,

A Gryphon, as drawn by Wilfred Dodgson upon whom
the Wonderland creature was based.

were in the boat. Wilfred, who was a good oarsman, certainly rowed for his brother on river trips with the Liddell children, as in a letter to Alice, written after his brother's death in 1898 (and which can be found in Christ Church library), he says:

> I may claim to have been long ago counted to some small extent amongst the friends of your childhood, and to have shared with my brother the pleasure of the excursions on the river when so many of his stories grew to maturity.

Wilfred left Oxford after obtaining his degree in 1860, so the river trips must have taken place that year or in the period from 1858 when Carroll's diaries are missing, but well before the main stories were told in 1862. In 'Alice's Recollections of Carrollian Days', published in *The Cornhill Magazine* in July 1932, the heroine of Wonderland remembered that many of the stories in the book took place before the all-important Godstow trip. She told a young friend, Ernest Odell of Lyndhurst, that everybody present on the trips featured as characters in the stories and it is not difficult to spot the part assigned to Wilfred in *Alice's Adventures in Wonderland*. Wilfred was a kindred spirit, whimsical and good at story-telling, who had contributed a blood-curdling poem to the *Rectory Umbrella*. Like his brother, he made drawings as stories proceeded, and his daughter, Menella, later confirmed that this made his story-telling special for his own children.

The reader of *Alice's Adventures in Wonderland* is told, 'If you don't know what a Gryphon is, look at the picture', and still to be found in the Christ Church library is an illustration of a Gryphon drawn by Wilfred for the story and initialled WLD. There are other clues about the identities of the Gryphon and the Mock Turtle: both went to the same school. The Gryphon, Wilfred, took Classics and was taught 'Laughing and Grief' by an old crab but the Mock Turtle, obviously Skeffington, took only the 'regular course'. Skeffington was indeed less bright than Wilfred and had to resit most of his exams: in 'The Two Brothers', a *Mischmasch* poem written in 1853 on the return of Skeffington and Wilfred from their prep school at Twyford, it had already been pointed out that one of them was 'too stupid for Greek and for Latin'. When the Mock Turtle was asked what else he learned besides arithmetic, he replied, counting off the subjects on his flappers, 'Mystery, ancient and modern, with Seaography: then Drawling – the Drawling-master was an old conger-eel, that used to come once a week: he taught us Drawling, Stretching, and Fainting in coils'. Alice could recognise in this sea school her own 'drawling-master', who came in once a week: he was none other than John Ruskin.

Although Twyford School was near Winchester, and not in the sea, it was of great interest to the Liddell children as their brother Harry was there at the time Carroll was telling the story about the 'best of educations' that the Wonderland school provided. (One wonders if the Twyford bills really did say at the end, 'French, music and washing extra'.) Carroll had tried, rather unsuccessfully, to coach Harry in the different branches of arithmetic – 'Ambition, Distraction, Uglification and Derision' – before he took the Twyford entrance exam, but had ended up taking him to the boat races instead. The Gryphon seems to understand, however, that what Alice really liked to hear about was what had been happening to her and, after a long session of antics with the Mock Turtle in the lobster-quadrille, he adds, 'Come, let's hear some of *your* adventures.'

15

IV

A Mad Tea-Party

The kind of Alice-orientated story the little girl particularly liked to hear was the nonsense account of her birthday party that appeared in *Wonderland* as 'A Mad Tea-Party', where the date of her birthday is, for all time, subtly revealed. At the end of the previous chapter, when she leaves the Cheshire cat and goes in search of the Mad Hatter and the March Hare, Alice hears herself saying, 'The March Hare will be much the most interesting, and perhaps, as this is May, it won't be raving mad – at least not so mad as it was in March,' and when they sit down at the tea-party, and the Hatter asks what day of the month it is, the storybook Alice considers a little, and then says, 'The fourth.' May 4, Alice's birthday, was a date Lewis Carroll remembered even after the child had become a woman and was referred to in his diary as 'Alice'.

May 4. 1871. On this day, 'Alice's' birthday, I sit down to record the events of the day

Alice, who always hoped that 'there will be some nonsense in it' when Mr Dodgson began his tales, was most likely aged eight, in 1860, at the fictitious mad birthday party. Twice in the Alice books the heroine tells us she is seven and a half, so perhaps we are to assume that is when her adventures began. Certainly the autumn term of 1859,

Illustration by Tenniel of 'A Mad Tea-Party'
held on Alice's birthday, 4 May.

when she was at Carroll's favourite age of seven, was a
momentous one for the Deanery and many of the early
stories must have been sparked off by its events. Queen
Victoria had decided to place the Prince of Wales under the
Dean's specific charge while he was at Oxford. The London
papers reported that 'the presence of the heir to the British
throne has excited considerable interest at this ancient seat
of learning'. The Prince came into residence on 17 October
1859 and the entire college turned out to line the quadrangle
in greeting, with all the Christ Church bells ringing. The
Dean proudly hailed him as the first Prince of Wales to have
entered Oxford since Henry V. Although the Prince, with
his Governor General Bruce and specially selected com-
panions, resided at his own establishment at Frewin Hall to
be visited there by his tutors, he attended cathedral services

regularly and made frequent visits to the Deanery, where the hour for dinner was changed to seven to suit his convenience. Although the Dean noted in his memoirs that he found him 'the nicest little fellow possible, so simple, naïf, ingenuous and modest', his academic aptitude was unimpressive and his tutor suggested that his knowledge of history might just as well have been acquired from Scott's novels. His parents were determined that he should benefit from his studies at Oxford and within a fortnight a check was made on progress. 'Dear Papa', wrote the Queen to the Princess Royal, 'has gone to Oxford to see how Bertie is going on in that old monkish place, which I have a horror of' (Fulford, 1964, p. 215).

A special banquet was given at Christ Church to celebrate the Heir Apparent's eighteenth birthday on 9 November 1859. Turtle soup was always on the menu on royal occasions and Christ Church children were known to have ridden on the turtles' backs before they were made into soup in the kitchen. The huge turtle shells were hung on the kitchen walls after the soup-making and the song 'Turtle Soup' in *Wonderland* would have special meaning for the children. Rather naturally, when called to sing the song, the Mock Turtle 'sighed deeply, and began in a voice choked with sobs, to sing thus:

> *"Beautiful Soup, so rich and green,*
> *Waiting in a hot tureen!"* '

This was a parody of 'Beautiful Star' which was included in the repertoire of songs that Alice and her sisters, Ina and Edith, often performed as a trio for visitors in the Deanery drawing room.

The royal year brought extra welcome treats for the Dean's

children. Magicians, minstrels, conjurors and all kinds of entertainers always converged on Oxford in term-time and, provided they obtained the Vice-Chancellor's permission, were allowed to advertise in the local press to attract the undergraduates. The pressure by the entertainers was stepped up while the Prince of Wales was in Oxford. Although Prince Albert, who thought his son was a 'thorough and cunning lazybones', had ordered that the Prince should be kept at his studies, HRH had made it known that he would like to attend some of these functions at the Town Hall and Star Assembly Rooms. To ensure the propriety of these entertainments, the Vice-Chancellor felt obliged to attend, accompanied by the Proctors and the 'bull dogs' (the university police). The newspapers reported that the best families in the county and university were now to be seen at these events, some of which were specifically under the patronage of the Dean of Christ Church. Mrs Liddell was never one to be left out and had the children with her whenever possible. The Prince's taste, like that of most Victorians, was broad, to say the least: musical evenings, military concerts, dioramas, minstrel singing, and all kinds of extravaganzas. Two performances he heard, with the Liddells present, were Christies minstrels singing 'Beautiful Star', and a ventriloquist of international fame, imitating a child repeating Watts's hymn 'How doth the little busy bee' which, according to the Oxford papers, had 'never been surpassed, if it has ever been equalled'. Carroll parodied this as 'How doth the little crocodile' recited by Alice after she has fallen down the rabbit-hole.

The entertainments that the Liddell children attended were undoubtedly discussed with Mr Dodgson the next time they saw him. It is unfortunate that the diaries are missing, so we are prevented from knowing which events he and his brothers, Wilfred and Skeffington, who were also up in the Prince's year, had seen. One performance Carroll would have wanted to see was that given on 3 May 1860 by the world-famous Russian Professor of Physical and Natural Magic, Wiljalba Frikell, as he himself was so greatly interested in magic. The Professor boasted that he needed no props nor long-sleeved theatrical attire for deception and appeared in evening dress making great play of his top hat from which he produced a seemingly endless array of objects – including a live goldfish. To show that the magic power did not lie within his own hat, the Professor called for the loan of a hat from the packed audience. There was thunderous applause when the Prince of Wales handed up his own topper from which more strange objects were produced.

It was very likely that Alice would have been taken by her parents to see Professor Frikell's magic for a birthday treat. The Senior Proctor, whose duty it was to witness any performance the royal alumnus attended, was Professor Bartholomew Price, formerly Carroll's tutor and leader of the Whitby reading party, and a great friend of the Liddells. He was an eminent mathematician with a keen interest in astronomy, whose lectures some undergraduates maintained were way over their heads. He was energetically involved with all the numerous Oxford committees and known throughout the university as 'Bat'. The significance of

> *"Twinkle, twinkle, little bat!*
> *How I wonder what you're at!*
> *Up above the world you fly,*
> *Like a tea-tray in the sky."*

sung at Alice's tea-party, would not have been lost on her.

In the Wonderland birthday party episode the Hatter is

wearing a topper prominently priced 10/6d (ten shillings and sixpence). Top hats were in great demand while the Prince was up at Oxford and at Easter 1860 Margetts of Cornmarket put a display of London toppers bearing the price tag '10/6d' in their shop window. Two letters in *The Times* in 1931 claimed that the Mad Hatter was Theophilus Carter, formerly a Christ Church servitor with ugly features, who was a furniture upholsterer at 49 High Street, and well known to Oxford as he used to stand at the door of his shop 'sometimes in an apron, always with a top hat at the back of his head'. Theophilus Carter invented 'The Alarm Clock Bed', exhibited at the Great Exhibition in 1851, which tipped its occupant out on to the floor at the hour for which the clock was set.

Time certainly dominates the Mad Tea-Party, and much effort is put into trying to wake up the Dormouse. Time was a subject that greatly intrigued Lewis Carroll, and he took it rather more seriously, of course, than the Mad Hatter. In November 1860 he gave a lecture on 'Where does the day begin?' to the Ashmolean Society, of which 'Bat' was a leading light. His argument, which he had already set out in the *Rectory Umbrella* and in a letter to *The Times*, was postulated before the date-line was instituted. It was summarised in the words of his nephew, Stuart Dodgson Collingwood:

> If a man could travel round the world so fast that the sun would be always directly above his head, and if he were to start midday on Tuesday, then in twenty-four hours he would return to his original point of departure, and would find that the day was now called Wednesday – at what point of his journey would the day change its name? (Collingwood, 1898, p. 85)

When it came to beating time Christ Church didn't help matters, for, as Alice knew, the college and cathedral kept different times from the rest of Oxford. After complaints from the town about the chimes of the college's Tom Tower, its clock was synchronised with Greenwich time. The cathedral, however, persisted in keeping the old local time (and still does).

V

Court Cards and Photography

Queen Victoria apparently overcame her horror of Oxford sufficiently to visit the Deanery on 12 December 1860, for a final check on her son's progress at end-of-term examinations. All the Liddell children, except perhaps Rhoda, who had only been born the year before, were invited to meet her. Fortunately, we have Carroll's diary entry for the occasion, as it is given in *The Life and Letters of Lewis Carroll* compiled by his nephew Stuart Dodgson Collingwood in 1898, before the 1860 diary was lost:

> Visit of the Queen to Oxford, to the great surprise of everybody, as it had been kept a secret up to the time. She arrived at Christ Church about twelve, and came into Hall with the Dean. . . . The party consisted of the Queen, Prince Albert, Princess Alice and her intended husband, the Prince of Hesse-Darmstadt, the Prince of Wales, Prince Alfred, and suite.

In a letter home Carroll admitted that he had never seen the Queen 'so near before, nor on her feet, and was shocked to find how short, not to say dumpy, and (with all loyalty be it spoken), how plain she is'. Alice, too, was seeing a queen close up for the first time and this must have been the main topic of conversation with Carroll as soon as she could find him. The Queen's visit also added a new interest to court cards when next they played their usual 'Beggar my

Neighbour' together, for frequently Carroll pretended that the pack of cards came to life. He invented his own game called 'Court Circular', the rules for which he published in 1860. Hearts ranked first in the game, but if anybody hinted at the imperious Queen of Hearts taking the Knave of Hearts to task or ordering people's heads to be chopped off, however, it would only have been done with the greatest loyalty and propriety.

Evening entertainment for the Prince of Wales was provided at the Deanery after the Queen's departure. He had come to know the Liddell children well and enjoyed their drawing-room performances. Alice he found good to tease. On one of his unexpected visits to the Deanery his arrival, when announced in the drawing room, had caused great consternation, as Mrs Liddell had deemed it safe for Alice to try on a new frock from the dressmaker. The petticoated Alice disappeared out of a side door leaving a trail of pins behind her, and her mother, not easily caught off her guard, stuffed the frock behind the sofa before making her formal curtsey. The Prince of Wales pretended not to have noticed, but when he took his leave he said slyly, 'Tell Alice I saw her.'

Carroll's diary entry for 12 December, recording the Queen's visit, goes on to describe the evening entertainment provided for the Prince of Wales:

> I went a little after half-past eight, and found a great party assembled – The Prince had not yet come. He arrived before nine, and I found an opportunity of reminding General Bruce of his promise to introduce me to the Prince, which he did at the next break in the conversation with Mrs Fellowes.

The Liddell children were preparing to give a tableau vivant performance of 'The Sleeping Princess' and the Prince told

24

Carroll that he had seen and admired his photographs of them. Carroll, who would have dearly loved to photograph the Prince of Wales, said he would be honoured if he would accept any of his photographs. He was invited to take his albums round to Frewin Hall and the Prince chose about a dozen, including two photographs of the Liddell children, in Chinese costume and in a cherry group, showing them acting out 'Open your mouth, and shut your eyes.'

Photography became popular after the Great Exhibition of 1851, when the wet or collodion process was developed for the use of the amateur. Charles Dodgson, who acquired his first camera in 1856, soon became accomplished at the art and would have made his name as a Victorian photographer if he had not become famous as Lewis Carroll. Being able to record child friends at the special moment of acquaintance was a great delight for, as he said, they would 'grow up so quick'. Carroll kept a register of the names and ages of the scores of children he photographed, with the date and number of the negative. After he moved to his upstairs set of rooms on the St Aldate's college front in 1868 he had a glass-house studio built on the roof. Most of his photographs of the Liddell children, including the two chosen by the Prince of Wales, were taken in 1858 and 1859 so that he could remember her for all time as 'an entirely fascinating little seven-year-old maiden'. Tennyson said that the one of Alice as a Beggar Child was the most beautiful portrait of a child he had ever seen.

Alice recalled in 1932 that, in spite of the length of time they had to sit still in those early days of amateur photography, having their pictures taken held no fears for her and her sisters as it went hand in hand with the story-telling.

'The Cherry Group' – one of Lewis Carroll's photographs chosen by the Prince of Wales. Edith is on the left, Ina in the middle and Alice on the right.

Mr Dodgson was one of the first amateur photographers, and took many photographs of us. In winter, when we could not go on the river, we used to go out of the back door of the Deanery, escorted by our nurse, and go to his rooms in the "Old Library". When we got there, we used to sit on the big sofa on each side of him, while he told us stories, illustrating them by pencil or ink drawings as he went along. When we were thoroughly happy and amused at his stories, he used to pose us, and expose the plates, before the right mood passed. He seemed to have an endless store of fantastical stories, which he made up as he told them, drawing busily on a large sheet of paper all the time. . . . Being photographed was therefore a joy to us and not a penance as it is to most children. We looked forward to the happy hours in the mathematical tutor's rooms.

Many children recalled how the smell of collodion hung about Carroll's rooms but Alice only remembered enjoying the sight of the large glass plates being developed in his dark room. Lewis Carroll kept a cupboard full of dressing-up clothes, which included a Turkish costume, a fairy prince outfit, a Greek dress and a suit of mail. Sometimes he would even send his scout (college servant) over to the Ashmolean to get some more authentic ethnic costume, such as that needed for the Professor of Sanskrit's small daughter, Ella, who was to be photographed as a sleeping savage and required a native cloak and anklet, or for Beatrice Hatch, who was to be a South Sea islander. The Chinese mandarin costume worn by Alice and Ina Liddell, which had taken the Prince's fancy, may have been bought from a pantomime sale.

Another aspect of the 'happy hours' that children spent with Lewis Carroll, apart from the nonsense tales, was his

Illustration by Tenniel of 'The Queen's croquet ground'. The cards have fallen flat on their faces at her approach. The Botanic Garden water-lily house can be seen in the background.

flair for unobtrusive instruction given on walks and while being photographed. This kind of palatable learning, common in every nursery school today, was unheard of in the 1860s. Something about the geography and customs of China would certainly have been studied and talked over with Alice and Ina before they dressed up in their Chinese costume. The best illustrated book of travels to China would have been Macartney's famous *Embassy to China*, which was, of course, in the Christ Church library and could have been borrowed for the session. John Barrow, the editor of Macartney's journals, made much of Macartney's visit to the Emperor, who was borne aloft on a gold palanquin and before whom everybody was forced to kowtow. When he appeared, Macartney wrote, 'Instantly the whole court fell flat on their faces' and perhaps Carroll and his little friends tried doing this. In *Alice's Adventures* the imperious Queen of Hearts, with her crown borne before her, orders the cards to prostrate themselves and the illustration shows how 'the three gardeners instantly threw themselves flat on their faces'. Added to the published *Alice's Adventures in Wonderland* is what Alice Liddell herself surely had said, with all the logical realism of a seven-year-old, when she first heard about the prostrating and kowtowing: ' "What would be the use of a procession," thought she, "if people had all to lie on their faces, so that they couldn't see it?" '

VI

'Happy Hours' with the 'Mathematical Tutor'

Walks round Oxford with Lewis Carroll – and Alice, Edith and Ina had many of these – were always a mixture of fun and education for the children. A favourite visit was to the Botanic Garden at the end of Broad Walk, where Professor Daubeny kept a wide range of exotic plants. His water-lily house, seen behind the Queen's croquet ground in Tenniel's illustration, was most popular with children. There were outings to see the deer in Magdalen Grove and to feed the ducks on the lake at Worcester College. The best place for nature study was Christ Church meadows, and one little girl, another Alice, who attributed her love of animals to Mr Dodgson and 'his stories of animal life, his knowledge of their lives and histories, his enthusiasm about birds and butterflies', recalled how he helped her to overcome her horror of the snails that appeared along the walls on the Merton Meadow walk by studying their discarded shells and collecting them in a little crimson trunk which he bought for her at the toy shop (Cohen, 1989, p. 175).

Walks with their governess, Miss Prickett, 'to let off steam', were a necessary part of the Liddell children's afternoon routine, since it was a strict rule that they should not run about in the quadrangle and disturb people. Miss Prickett's family lived at Binsey, a nearby village reached along the Thames tow-path, and on fine days the children were

Drawn & Eng.d by J. & H. Storer.

View from
CHRIST CHURCH WALK.

Entrance to Broad Walk leading to Christ Church and Merton meadows, the scene of many 'happy hours' of walks with Lewis Carroll and instruction in natural history. Tom Tower is in the background.

31

sometimes taken there. St Frideswide's holy well at Binsey has a special connection with both Oxford and *Wonderland*. Alice had been brought up on the story of Oxford's patron saint, in whose honour the Dean preached the St Frideswide sermon each year on her festival, 19 October. The Saint's shrine is in the cathedral, which is built on the site of the monastery she founded, and in 1860 a St Frideswide's window, commissioned by Alice's father and painted by Burne-Jones, was dedicated. All Christ Church had watched the glass panels, showing scenes in the Saint's life, being assembled on the grass behind the Latin chapel. One of the panels portrayed the Binsey holy well, miraculously called forth by St Frideswide, with a sign post ('Oxford–Binsey') linking the two places of pilgrimage in the Middle Ages.

The holy well had always been called the treacle well by local people, still using the word treacle in its biblical sense of a healing fluid. The story of the treacle well is told by the Dormouse at Alice's mad birthday tea-party, which has other overtones of 1860, the year that the St Frideswide's window inspired renewed interest in Oxford's patron saint and her holy well.

"Once upon a time there were three little sisters ... and their names were Elsie [L C – Lorina Charlotte], Lacie [Alice], and Tillie [Edith's pet name]; and they lived at the bottom of a well."

When Alice, rather naturally, asked why these three little girls should live at the bottom of a well, she was told it was a 'treacle' well. ' "There's no such thing," ' Alice was beginning to say but then she remembered that there might be one after all.

Walks with their governess were all very well, but the

children were delighted when Mr Dodgson was free from
his mathematics and could accompany them and make up
stories about the things they saw. The gargoyles on the college walls were great fun and Lewis Carroll liked to point
out the large, jolly face at the top of a wall at Magdalen
College which is being helped to laugh by a little man
pulling up the corners of his mouth for him. He had been
fascinated as a child by carvings in his father's churches at
Daresbury and Croft, and later, when his father became
Archdeacon, by the work of the famous carvers of Ripon,
who depicted knights in battle, pigs playing bagpipes and
lions fighting dragons in the cathedral. Alice told him how
she pretended that the carved lions on the Deanery staircase
came alive and chased her down the long gallery to her
nursery. These new carved Gothic stairs had been paid for
by the profits from her father's Greek Lexicon, the well-
known 'Liddell and Scott', and the children had christened
them 'the Lexicon stairs'. Once when Mr Dodgson took
Alice round the University Press on one of their walks, the
dictionary was being set in type for its sixth edition.

The Liddell children took a lively interest in all that went
on in Oxford and they were honoured guests at any university institution. Their father, as well as being a Delegate of
the Press, was a Curator of the Bodleian Library, a Delegate
of the University Museum and Art Galleries and a Curator
of the Chest (that is, a member of the university's finance
committee). Dean Liddell was involved in all the reforms
and enterprises which made the Oxford of the 1860s such a
lively intellectual centre, and Mrs Liddell was renowned for
her evening parties for distinguished guests. The Deanery
was not the kind of Victorian household where children
were banished to the nursery (Alice had been about to point

out to the sea creatures in *Wonderland* that she had tasted grown-up food like lobster, but had thought better of it). Alice and her sisters often stayed up for parties, contributed to the entertainment, like the tableaux vivants for the Prince of Wales, or played parlour games with bishops and professors. Alice knew most of the Oxford professors, and not just 'Bat', since they were the only resident members of the university, other than Heads of Houses and the Canons of Christ Church, who were allowed to marry, and most of her friends were the children of professors. Alice was very familiar with academics who talked like the egg-headed Humpty Dumpty sitting on a high Oxford stone wall or who were ready to give philosophical advice, like the Caterpillar smoking a hookah pipe on a toadstool.

The University Museum, opened in 1860, was a splendid new place to visit. It was the brainchild of John Ruskin and Sir Henry Acland, the Regius Professor of Medicine, both former pupils of Dean Liddell, who gave the project his wholehearted support. Acland was the Liddell family doctor and Ruskin was Alice's drawing master, the 'old conger eel, that used to come once a week'. Alice and her sisters liked to look at the stuffed animals and birds, especially if Mr Dodgson was there to make up fantastical stories about them. The upstairs galleries housed the Hope collection of crustaceans and insects, duly classified, but what the storybook Alice, who like her namesake was also rather afraid of insects, 'really wanted to know was whether it could sting or not'.

A favourite exhibit in the main hall was the remains of the strange dodo, which had been brought to Oxford in 1683 with the rest of the Tradescant Collection of Rarities, and which bore the label 'The Head and Foot of the last living

Dodo seen in Europe'. Substitution bones had replaced those missing so that, as the catalogue claimed, from the remains, being exhibited beside a very accurate painting of a Dodo, 'naturalists are able to describe the bird very definitely. It belongs to the Pigeon family.' The extinction of an inept species was of great interest in Oxford, following the famous British Association meeting of 1860, when the great debate on Darwinian theory had taken place in the newly finished museum, which is commemorated by a plaque in the Upper West Gallery. Carroll had been on the reception committee for the 'men of science from foreign countries and distant parts of the UK'. His own contribution to the burning question of evolution was the invention of a game called Natural Selection in which the winner demonstrated the theory of the 'survival of the fittest'. The dodo, however, was to get a new lease of life when it appeared in *Wonderland*, as it was with this strange, obsolete creature that Lewis Carroll chose to identify himself as a character in *Alice's Adventures*.

Another creature that appears to be left over from the great debate is the monkey which is seen in the illustrations of *Alice's Adventures*. Oxford was electrified and one lady fainted and was carried out of the room after the fundamentalist Bishop of Oxford, Samuel Wilberforce, had sneeringly asked the biologist Thomas Huxley whether he claimed his descent from a monkey through his grandmother or grandfather and Huxley had indicated that he would prefer to be descended from a monkey than a bishop. Carroll's reactions are not recorded as his diary is missing, but he took care to arrange to take a photograph of Huxley. The undergraduates found it all very hilarious and flocked to a lecture at the Star Assembly Rooms entitled 'Can a Man be a Monkey?', which was presented by an African traveller, accompanied on the platform by a stuffed gorilla. The theory of evolution was over Alice's head, of course, although doubtless there was much discussion of the debate at the Deanery, maybe even with the Bishop himself, but whenever she went to the Botanic Gardens she liked to take nuts and biscuits along to feed the monkeys that Professor Daubeny, a committed Huxleyite, kept in the cages in the Danby Gateway.

The really special outings were the river trips which Alice said took place four or five times during the summer term. On 6 August 1862, Lewis Carroll noted that Ina, who was three years older than Alice and tall for her age, had already been on fourteen such trips and might not be allowed to come again. Ina's first trip, when she was only seven, and accompanied by her nine-year-old brother Harry, was recorded in Carroll's diary as a very special occasion even though Alice's adventures had not yet begun. Carroll's cousin, Frank Smedley, was also in the party.

> June 5. 1856. From 4.30 to 7 Frank and I made a boating excursion with Harry and Ina: the latter, much to my surprise, having got permission from the Dean to come. We went down to the island, and made a kind of picnic there, taking biscuits with us, and buying ginger beer and lemonade there. Harry as before rowed stroke most of the way, and fortunately, considering the wild spirits of the children, we got home without accidents, having attracted by our remarkable crew a good deal of attention from almost everyone we met. Mark this day, annalist, not only with a white stone, but as altogether 'Dies mirabilis'.

VII

The Pool of Tears and the Caucus-race

We know that there must have been many trips in the years of the missing diaries but we can only follow the Liddell children again on their river excursions from 9 May 1862, a few days after Alice's tenth birthday, when Carroll's diaries begin again. From then on we can identify, with more certainty, some of the events that turned into Alice's fantastical adventures. Harry was no longer present, as he was away at his prep school in Twyford, but Edith was old enough to join in. The first river excursion with the children recorded in the new volume was on 26 May, but this did not take them very far, only just down the river to Iffley, where Carroll and the other oarsman, Reginald Southey, his photographer friend, decided to abandon it because of the strong current and they all went off for a game of croquet in the Deanery garden. The next trip, on 17 June, provoked a whole chapter in *Alice's Adventures* and Carroll records the episode, which took place while his sisters Fanny and Elizabeth were staying in Oxford, in some detail:

> June 17. (Tu.) Expedition to Nuneham. Duckworth (of Trinity) and Ina, Alice and Edith came with us. We set out about 12.30 and got to Nuneham about 2: dined there, then walked in the park and set off for home about 4.30. About a mile above Nuneham heavy rain came on, and after bearing it a short time I settled that we had better leave

37

> the boat and walk: three miles of this drenched us
> all pretty well. I went on first with the children,
> as they walk much faster than Elizabeth, and
> took them to the only house I know in Sandford,
> Mrs. Broughton's, where Ranken lodges. I left
> them with her to get their clothes dried, and went
> off to find a vehicle, but none was to be had
> there, so on the others arriving, Duckworth and I
> walked on to Iffley, whence we sent them a fly.
> We all had tea in my rooms about 8.30, after
> which I took the children home.

Alice recalled that this was a sombre occasion and that
there was none of the usual story-telling prompted by the
children's hilarity, as they were too awed by the 'old ladies',
who, although only in their early thirties, seemed 'dreadful-
ly old' to them.

> On one occasion two of Mr Dodgson's sisters joined the
> party, making seven of us, all in one boat. They seemed to
> us rather stout, and one might have expected that, with such
> a load in it, the boat would have been swamped. However, it
> was not the river that swamped us but the rain. It came on to
> pour so hard that we had to land at Iffley, and after trying to
> dry the Misses Dodgson at a fire, we drove home.

Robinson Duckworth, a keen member of the University
amateurs, had done his best while they were still being
drenched in the boat, by singing his usual popular songs,
'Star of the Evening', 'Twinkle, twinkle, little star' and
'Will you walk into the parlour'. The whole sequence of
events was to be remembered on the next river trip, the
all-important one to Godstow, when it could be recalled
with the children's usual high spirits encouraging the nonsense elements, and undampened by rain or the presence of

Illustration by Tenniel of the Dodo giving Alice a prize.
Carroll identified himself with the Dodo in the University Museum.
Among the birds, a monkey is clearly visible.

intimidating ladies. Clearly Alice had been teased about adding to the wetness of the last occasion by crying as when the fictional Alice is confronted by the pool of tears she wishes she 'hadn't cried so much'. The other participants in the retold story of the drenching were 'a Duck and a Dodo, a Lory and an Eaglet, and several other curious creatures' – the Duck being Duckworth, the Dodo Dodgson, the Lory Lorina (Ina Liddell), and an Eaglet Alice's younger sister Edith. Also in the illustration appears what seems to be a Daubeny monkey. The Mouse, 'who seemed to be a person of some authority among them' was clearly Carroll's sister Frances, the eldest of the family and four years his senior, of whom the children were in awe.

It was the Mouse who had told them the driest pieces of history in an attempt to dry them off. Frances seems to have been keen on history as in one of his letters home Carroll had asked if she had finished reading Alison's *Europe*. The Dodgsons were proud of their Northumbrian ancestry and Carroll recorded in his diary in 1856 that he had spent some time in the Christ Church library searching the name of Dodgson in indexes to county histories. The family tree could be traced back to William the Conqueror, a Dodgson forebear having married Matilda, William's illegitimate daughter. The Mouse reeled off in her driest voice: 'William the Conqueror, whose cause was favoured by the pope, was soon submitted to by the English, who wanted leaders, and had been of late much accustomed to usurpation and conquest. Edwin and Morcar, the earls of Mercia and Northumbria – ' but although everybody was getting terribly bored, they were as wet as ever and, as we read in *Alice's Adventures Under Ground*, the manuscript version of Alice's adventures not originally intended for publication:

After a time the Dodo became impatient, and, leaving the Duck to bring up the rest of the party, moved on at a quicker pace with Alice, the Lory, and the Eaglet, and soon brought them to a little cottage, and there they sat snugly by the fire, wrapped in blankets, until the rest of the party had arrived and they were all dry again.

By the time Alice had recovered her spirits the creatures had started to move off and she said to herself:

I do wish some of them had stayed a little longer! and I was getting to be such friends with them – really the Lory and I were almost like sisters! and so was that dear little Eaglet! And then the Duck and the Dodo! How nicely the Duck sang to us as we came along the water: and if the Dodo hadn't known the way to that nice little cottage, I don't know when we should have got dry again.

The story was exactly like the real event and would have been enjoyed by Alice in the book that Carroll wrote for her. However, when he came to publish *Under Ground* as *Alice's Adventures in Wonderland* he took out the piece about the cottage and, when the Mouse's driest pieces of history did not help to dry them, the Dodo instead suggested that 'the best thing to get us dry would be a Caucus-race'. In this they could all run round in circles, as they did at university caucus meetings, and get themselves dry again. Carroll hated intrigue, wire-pulling and canvassing, the soul of Oxford politics, and parodied a caucus in his skit on *The Elections to the Hebdomadal Council*, which he published in 1866 (the Council was, as it were, the Cabinet of the University). The *Wonderland* caucus-race seemed to dry them off all right and everyone won a prize at the end of the race, with Alice having to produce a box of comfits and a thimble from her own pocket as

41

prizes – the latter being solemnly handed back to her as her own prize. In Tenniel's illustration, when the Dodo, alias Carroll, presents Alice with the thimble his sleeve shows he is wearing an academic gown.

VIII

The Golden Afternoon

The next river excursion planned after Carroll's sisters had left Oxford was for 3 July, but as on this occasion the rain came on before they set out, they stayed at the Deanery where the children sang songs, one of which was 'Sally come up! Sally go down!', which Carroll noted they sang 'with great spirit'. The weather cleared up enough for Duckworth to join them at croquet later in the afternoon, and in spite of the disappointment of not going on the river, the day was much enjoyed by Carroll as he ends the entry, 'I mark this day with a white stone.' This would have meant an afternoon when there had been special rapport with the children and much fun, good humour and fantasy story-telling, soon to be woven into *Alice's Adventures*. Was this the occasion when Carroll made the croquet mallets come to life as flamingoes, and the balls turn into hedgehogs, a story to be reworked the next day when the weather cleared and the postponed excursion could take place? Doubtless Alice's cat, Dinah, sat on the horizontal bough of the chestnut tree and watched them with a broad grin on her face.

Carroll's Cambridge friend, Francis Atkinson, was staying with him to help edit *College Rhymes* and narrowly missed going on the river trip which might have earned him a place in literature. It was 'the Duck' again who was to be the *Wonderland* oarsman. This time, when they took their boat from Folly Bridge, they headed up the river to

Godstow, about three miles away, passing by Binsey and its treacle well. Duckworth was in good form: he parodied 'Sally come up', sung so beautifully by the children the previous day, as 'Salmon come up' in the 'Lobster Quadrille'. Carroll's diary entry for the Godstow trip reads:

> July 4. (F) . . . Duckworth and I made an expedition up the river to Godstow with the three Liddells: we had tea on the bank there, and did not reach Christ Church again till quarter past eight, when we took them to my rooms to see my collection of micro-photographs, and restored them to the Deanery just before nine.

Later he added: 'On which occasion I told them the fairy-tale of "Alice's Adventures Underground" ' and Alice confirmed in her 'Recollections' that 'Nearly all of "Alice's Adventures Underground" was told on that blazing summer afternoon with the heat haze shimmering over the meadows where the party landed to shelter for a while in the shadow cast by the haycocks near Godstow.'

The best place to picnic was right by the lock at Godstow near the old abbey on farm land with plenty of haycocks. Across the Thames was a backwater with eel traps, the very place to parody 'Old Father William' with an eel on his nose. Balancing and somersaulting were very much in the children's minds as a few days before they had been taken to see the great French acrobat Charles Blondin perform on Holywell Green and had there met Lewis Carroll and his guest, Francis Atkinson. Blondin had set up a low rope and showed the fascinated Oxonians, and none more so than Carroll and the Liddell children, the feats he had performed over Niagara, sometimes blindfolded, in a sack, trundling a wheel-barrow, turning somersaults on stilts with prongs on the end, balancing chairs on his head, carrying a man on his back and sitting down halfway while he made and ate an omelette. However could he do it, and really at his age was it right?

This special Godstow trip was recorded not only in *Under Ground*, but in later years by Alice, Duckworth and Carroll himself when writing about 'Alice on the Stage' in *The Theatre*, April 1887. Carroll also published three poems in memory of the story-telling on that 'golden afternoon', one of which is an acrostic of Alice's full name with the initial letters of the lines spelling out Alice Pleasance Liddell.

> *A Boat, beneath a sunny sky*
> *Lingering onward dreamily*
> *In an evening of July —*
> *Children three that nestle near,*
> *Eager eye and willing ear,*
> *Pleased a simple tale to hear —*
> *Long has paled that sunny sky:*
> *Echoes fade and memories die:*
> *Autumn frosts have slain July*
> *Still she haunts me, phantomwise.*
> *Alice moving under skies*
> *Never seen by waking eyes.*
> *Children yet, the tale to hear,*
> *Eager eye and willing ear,*
> *Lovingly shall nestle near.*
> *In a Wonderland they lie,*
> *Dreaming as the days go by,*
> *Dreaming as the summers die:*
> *Ever drifting down the stream —*
> *Lingering in the golden gleam —*
> *Life, what is it but a dream?*

Father William illustration by Tenniel. The famous picnic took place at Godstow on 4 July 1862. The eel traps on the Thames backwater can be seen on the right.

Usually, on these river trips with the Liddell children, stories lived and died in Carroll's words 'like summer midges', but on this 'golden afternoon' the rabbit-hole story was told all the way and continued through the Godstow picnic. The day was to have an important ending, for these stories were not to die like summer midges. When Alice bade her friends goodnight at the Deanery door she said, according to Duckworth, ' "Oh, Mr Dodgson, I wish you would write out Alice's adventures for me",' and 'he said he would try, and afterwards told me that he sat up nearly the whole night, committing to a MS book his recollections of the drolleries with which he had enlivened the afternoon.' The next day he recorded in his diary:

> July 5. Left, with Atkinson, for London at 9.2, meeting at
> the station the Liddells who went up by the same
> train. [Elsewhere he noted that the headings for
> *Alice's Adventures Under Ground* were written out
> on his way to London that day]

Everything Carroll did was done to perfection and the idea of how to present the story remained in his head for some time, before he finally recorded it in his diary four months later:

> Nov. 13. Began writing the fairy-tale for Alice, which I told
> them July 4, going to Godstow – I hope to finish it
> by Christmas.

This was not to be, as he was dissatisfied with his illustrations. It was not until two years later that the book was finally sent to Alice on 26 November 1864, beautifully inscribed on the back cover – 'A Christmas Gift to a Dear Child in memory of a Summer Day' – in Mr Dodgson's neat handwriting and with his own evocative illustrations.

IX

Illustrations and Publication

Illustrations for Alice's book were essential, for, right at the beginning of the story, we are told that Alice has no use for a book 'without pictures or conversations', and these pictures would have to be, like those tossed off during story-telling, an integral part of the book. On 10 March 1863, Carroll records that he 'called at the Deanery . . . to borrow a Natural History to help in illustrating "Alice's Adventures".' This may have been one of the Dean's books, but there were plenty of natural history books in the college library, so it was more likely to have been from Alice's schoolroom, probably Cassell's popular *Natural History* which had just been published in parts. The creatures from that would have made Alice feel at home in Wonderland, where she could find herself 'in friendly chat with bird or beast'.

There was a long time to go before Carroll was satisfied with his drawings, particularly of the heroine herself, and one cannot imagine Alice (who, in the text, was so demanding that 'there ought to be a book written about me, that there ought') waiting patiently for two years to see the final illustrated version of her adventures. Doubtless she saw the manuscript when the text was completed at the beginning of 1863. Carroll himself said that by December it had been 'read and liked by so many children, and I have been so often asked to publish it, that I have decided on doing so'. One of those who saw it was Annie Rogers, the daughter of the Professor of Political Economy, whose seventh birthday party Carroll attended on 15 February 1863. Annie, who went on to be a great champion of women's educational rights, recalled later in *The Times* in 1928, when she was a tutor at St Hugh's College, that she had already seen the manuscript before receiving one of the first presentation copies of the published book.

What appears to have finally persuaded Carroll to have the manuscript published, however, was the reaction to the stories of his friend, George Macdonald, himself a children's writer, and the Macdonald family. We actually have the enthusiastic response from one of the children, young Greville, to whom it was read by his mother:

> When she came to the end I, being six, exclaimed that there ought to be 60,000 volumes of it. Certainly it was our enthusiasm that persuaded our Uncle Dodgson . . . to present the English-speaking world with one of its classics.

Having made the decision to publish, Carroll consulted his friend, Thomas Combe, the University Printer, and asked for the book to be printed at his own expense. The printing press, which hitherto had concentrated on Bibles and dictionaries, had been revitalised by 'Bat' Price, supported by Alice's father, with the appointment of Alexander Macmillan to act as publisher and distributor. While Carroll was still working on the pen and ink drawings for Alice's own manuscript book, he began to try out drawing on wood in order to make a wood block for printing, as he hoped that his own illustrations, which he felt were inextricably linked with Alice's adventures, could be used.

Carroll, who was very interested in art and regularly visited art galleries and exhibitions, had met most of the

Some of Carroll's trial illustrations for the wood blocks.

Pre-Raphaelites in Oxford. He had always hoped that he could improve his own drawing even though John Ruskin had told him that his talent was not sufficient to merit devoting much time to it. Carroll called on Combe, the Pre-Raphaelite's patron, again to show him his first attempt at drawing on wood. He also met the sculptor and a founder of the Pre-Raphaelite Brotherhood, Thomas Woolner, who was not very complimentary about his work and told him that he should learn to draw from life. However, Carroll persevered with the idea of illustrating *Alice* and sought advice from a Mr Jewitt in Camden Town, who was to do the wood-engraving for him. Whole days of the 1863 long vacation were spent photographing in London, not only portraits but works of Pre-Raphaelite art, including Alexander Munro's statuary and Rossetti's drawings, which made a deep impression on him. That summer he received Arthur Hughes's, 'The Girl with the Lilacs', which had been specially painted for him to hang in his rooms at Christ Church. The image of the heroine Carroll was then trying to illustrate was clearly influenced by Rossetti and Hughes, and the child who emerges is not the real perky little Alice with the dark brown fringe of the photographs but one with a soulful Pre-Raphaelite look and long crinkly hair (only at the end of the book did he attempt to draw the real Alice but then covered it up with her photograph, as seen on page 97). The Pre-Raphaelite imagery of the transient innocence of childhood is very apparent in Carroll's poetry and photography. For him Alice was 'the child of the pure unclouded brow, and dreaming eyes of wonder'. He was particularly interested in the way the visionary poet William Blake had woven together, almost like a medieval illumination, his words and drawings on this idea in *Songs of Innocence*.

51

Carroll does not record when he realised, resignedly, that a professional illustrator would be needed, but in January 1864, he arranged, through the editor of *Punch*, Tom Taylor, to meet John Tenniel, whose illustrations of animals for an edition of *Aesop's Fables* and his work as a *Punch* artist Carroll admired. Fortunately, Tenniel agreed to illustrate *Alice's Adventures* and there could have been no better choice; indeed it is difficult to think of *Alice* without Tenniel's line drawings, so perfectly do they match the Carroll imagination, with the right note of matter-of-factness to pin down the nonsense tales. Carroll had now finished his own illustrations, and *Under Ground* only needed the final touches before being presented to Alice. In her 'Recollections' Alice said that Tenniel used Carroll's drawings as the basis for his own illustrations and that they had 'frequent consultations' about them. Alice in the pool of tears or playing croquet with a flamingo are clearly recognisable from *Under Ground*, but Tenniel could call on a large *Punch* stock-in-trade, if a water-lily house or a chapter-house door were required. There was much discussion about a model for Alice and Tenniel was sent a favoured photograph of Canon Badcock of Ripon's daughter Mary. Tenniel, who was no Pre-Raphaelite, said that he no more needed a model than Carroll needed a multiplication table to work out a mathematical problem. He did take on many of Carroll's suggestions, however, and got used to receiving such notes as 'Don't give Alice so much crinoline' as work progressed.

Carroll wanted the illustrations for the published book to be as tightly woven into the text as they were in his own family magazines or in *Under Ground* where the child reader is told, 'If you don't know what a Gryphon is look at

The Mouse's tail as pasted up by Carroll as a guide for the printer.

the picture,' which was, of course, set into the text. Macmillan, the publisher, was given exact measurements and instructions as to how the forty-two illustrations should be inset, whether centrally or to the side, left or right of the page. Bill the Lizard being propelled up the chimney was to shoot 5 inches up the page, Alice's neck was to grow up $5\frac{1}{8}$ inches and the Cheshire cat's grin was to be ten lines high. The text was to be close to the illustration which related to it and that was how it stayed in the many reprints of the original edition. For the Mouse's Tail (in the Caucus-race chapter) Carroll asked the printer to set it in ever-decreasing sizes of type and his own pasted-up guide for the printer can still be seen: another example of his constant search for perfection. He ran into difficulties with the tail, however, when a French version was required.

After much thought, the title *Alice's Adventures in Wonderland* was finally chosen for the published version. The book was to be nearly twice as long as the manuscript, with two extra chapters, 'A Mad Tea-Party' and 'Pig and Pepper', and a much extended trial scene in 'Alice's Evidence'. Alice's naïve remarks are bolstered by *Punch* humour in the published Alice books. Carroll was a devoted reader of *Punch* and kept cuttings in a special book. The 1863 issues of *Punch* magazines, when Carroll was so pre-occupied with his published text, are full of Carrollian-type humour. The inspiration of the 'Pig and Pepper' chapter may have been from *Punch*. Professor Pepper's ghost illusions were the sensation of the year and were included in a show of physical and natural magic, billed as 'Two Hours in Wonder World' in Oxford in June 1863. *Punch* makes much of Professor Pepper with remarks such as 'Giving us Pepper', a skit by an alleged assistant, and 'He who peppers

"To answer the door?" he said. "What's it been asking of?"
He was so hoarse that Alice could scarcely hear him.

Tenniel's illustration of Alice's father's chapter-house door.
Alice had just begun to learn ballet and she is often seen in ballet positions.

most highly is certain to please'. *Punch* had a section on 'Cutting Remarks' such as, 'the gentleman who caught a train is recovering' or for their many clerical readers 'a Fish ordinary will be nominated to any vacant See'. Carroll's best cutting remark is that by the Joint of Mutton at the banquet, who says to Alice, 'It isn't etiquette to cut anyone you've been introduced to', a remark superbly illustrated by Tenniel, the *Punch* artist. The dialogue outside the chapter-house door is also pure *Punch*.

X

'Let's Pretend we're Kings and Queens'

Alice's adventures, so long as she and Carroll were together, continued as an 'interminable fairy-tale', even after the highlight of the 'golden afternoon' trip to Godstow. The next year, 1863, which saw Carroll so busy with finishing the manuscript of the story of *Alice's Adventures Under Ground* and arranging for its publication as *Wonderland*, was a time of special closeness with the Liddell children, inspiring renewed story-telling. These stories, however, were not written down at the time and remained in Carroll's head, and it was only in August 1866 that he told Macmillan he had 'a floating idea of writing a sort of sequel to Alice'. The nonsense of *Through the Looking-Glass, and what Alice found there* was composed in intervals between writing mathematics books. At Ripon, in January 1868, he recorded in his diary that he had 'written almost all of the pamphlet on Euclid V by Algebra' and 'also added a few pages to the 2nd volume of Alice'. He took steps to publish the second Alice book only in June 1868, when Tenniel finally agreed to do the illustrations. Carroll knew that, as with *Wonderland*, the illustrations were vital to the successful outcome of the book but, with the memory of the exacting relationship of the *Wonderland* partnership, it had taken Tenniel some time to agree to undertake a second volume. This time Tenniel was in a better position to put across his own ideas and even succeeded in persuading Carroll to scrap one whole chapter of the book, to be called 'The Wasp in a Wig', which he said he didn't find very interesting and 'altogether beyond the appliances of art' to illustrate.

When Alice received the first copy of *Through the Looking-Glass* at Christmas in 1871 she had long ceased to beg Carroll for stories. She would have been nineteen years old, with her hair up, when she relived the tales she had inspired eight years before. As Carroll said in the introductory poem it was 'a tale begun in other days . . . whose echoes live in memory yet' and inevitably it has a more nostalgic note. It is also more sophisticated: this time Carroll wrote the book with publication in mind. Gone is the extempore sparkle of *Wonderland*, the laughter of the children, the Duck's singing, the sound of the oars on the water and the interrupted stories fresh from the author's mouth. The story is set within the framework of chess, which the children had just begun to learn. The chess pieces are much more real than the cards in *Wonderland*; throughout there is a continuous thread of Alice, the pawn, making a series of moves until she finally becomes a queen, an allegory of her growing up.

Eighteen sixty-three was a very special royal year for the Liddell family and a highlight in the children's lives. It was the year of the wedding of the Prince of Wales, whose time at Christ Church was remembered with special affection by the Liddells. He and his young princess, Alexandra, were to spend three days at the Deanery as part of the celebrations. 'Let's pretend we're Kings and Queens', which Alice had been playing with her sister in the opening chapter of *Through the Looking-Glass*, sets the royal theme of the book. When Alice dozes off in the armchair with her kitten, the real royal event that had been uppermost in her mind turns into a fantasy game of chess in which kings and queens show her how to make the right moves to become a queen herself. ' "Do you know what tomorrow is, Kitty?" she had said before her dream adventures in Looking-Glass world overtook her. "You'd have guessed if you'd been up in the window with me – only Dinah was making you tidy, so you couldn't. I was watching the boys getting in sticks for the bonfire – and it wants plenty of sticks, Kitty. Only it got so cold, and it snowed so, they had to leave off. Never mind, Kitty, we'll go and see the bonfire tomorrow." '

All Oxford, both town and gown, were making elaborate preparations to celebrate the wedding of the Prince of Wales on 10 March. The previous day was bitterly cold, as Alice had observed in *Through the Looking-Glass*, when she watched the undergraduates making the Christ Church bonfire. It was, in fact, the coldest day of the winter with a minimum temperature of 25.7° Fahrenheit recorded at the Radcliffe Observatory, but, although still cold, the great day dawned bright and sunny. In the morning, the Liddells conducted an official planting of trees at the Cherwell end of Broad Walk. Lewis Carroll and his brother Edwin, who had come over from Rugby for the celebrations, watched the three Deanery children perform the ceremony. Carroll's diary records:

> Each delivered a short speech over her tree. 'Long life to this tree and may it prosper from this auspicious day' and they named them Alexandra, Albert and Victoria.

(Alexandra, Albert and Victoria, along with all the other elms in Broad Walk, succumbed to Dutch Elm Disease and were felled in 1977.)

The illuminations were the highlight of the Royal

Wedding Day celebrations and great crowds of people made a tour of the town after dark. Arrangements were being made for each of the Liddell children to have an escort to accompany them, but for Alice there was only one escort who would do justice to the tour of the illuminations, bonfires and fireworks by making it part of her adventures. She had accordingly sent a note round to Carroll's rooms the night before to ask if he would take her. As always, Carroll complied with alacrity to Alice's request, and it proved to be a memorable event in both their lives, marked in his diary with a white stone.

> After Hall we went to the Deanery for the children, and set out. We soon lost the others, and Alice and I with Edwin, took the round of all the principal streets in about two hours, bringing her home by half past nine. The mob was dense, but well conducted – the fireworks abundant, and some of the illuminations very beautiful. It was delightful to see the thorough abandonment with which Alice enjoyed the whole thing. The Wedding of the Prince of Wales I mark with a white stone.

The Oxford newspapers were loud in their praise for the ingenuity of the citizens and the colleges and the enterprise of the Gas Company, which had its own splendid star shining outside the city. Another huge star hung from the top of New College Tower, Wadham displayed a ten-foot plume and the Town Hall was resplendent with the City's arms; other buildings were decorated with true lovers' knots, and banners bearing slogans such as 'Those whom God hath joined together'. Christ Church, as befitted the royal foundation and the Prince of Wales's own college, was particularly festive and earned special commendation. On the St Aldate's front were three large stars, from 1200 gas jets, and a replica of Cardinal Wolsey's hat; there were lamps all round the quads, and along the side fronting Oriel was a transparency of the Prince of Wales's feathers and the initials of the happy pair lit up. But what was most admired by the Oxonians, and not the least of these was Alice from her vantage point at the Deanery's upstairs windows, was a large, beautiful, revolving crown in variegated lamps, high up on top of the Canterbury gate entrance to Christ Church.

The crown so persistently in Alice's thoughts is a recurring theme in *Through the Looking-Glass* and much of the imagery of the Lion and the Unicorn chapter relates to the royal celebrations.

> *The Lion and the Unicorn were fighting for the Crown;*
> *The Lion beat the Unicorn all round the town.*

The Lion and the Unicorn, the royal supporters, have stepped down from the royal coat of arms, everywhere to be seen, and amidst the noise and dust are fighting their way round the town but, as the White King points out, you need to know which way to go round the town to get the best view of it all. The weary lion at the end of the day could only speak to Alice in 'a deep hollow tone that sounded like the tolling of a great bell'. The great bell that played such a part in Alice's life was, of course, Great Tom at Christ Church. She used to listen to it in bed every night as it boomed 101 times for curfew at five past nine to commemorate the number of students on the original foundation. When Alice returned to Christ Church after the tour of the illuminations with Carroll it had already finished striking and she was handed back to the Deanery, tired but very happy. Alice could recall, even seventy years later, that the day after this exciting adventure, Carroll had sent her a

The Lion and the Unicorn, who have stepped out of the royal coat of arms.
Tenniel shows a skyline like that of St Aldate's opposite Christ Church.

caricature of one of the illuminations, 'May they be happy',
which had particularly taken her fancy and she much regret-
ted that it had been destroyed by her mother. 'It is an awful
thought to contemplate what may have perished in the
Deanery waste-paper basket,' lamented the recipient of so
many more of Carroll's lost nonsense treasures.

XI

Looking-Glass House

Mrs Liddell was expecting a baby at the end of March and arrangements were made for the children to be sent away to the Dean's mother at Hetton Lawn, Charlton Kings, near Cheltenham, with their governess. The visit to the grandmother's house with the great gilded looking-glass mirror over the drawing room mantelpiece was to play an important role in the sequel to *Wonderland* (at one time Carroll had thought of calling the book *Alice's Visit to Looking-Glass House*). Carroll had made plans to spend the Easter vacation with relations at Tenby and was pleased to receive an invitation from old Mrs Liddell to break his journey at Cheltenham and have lunch at Hetton Lawn.

> April 4 (Sat) Left Oxford by the 7.30. and reached Cheltenham by 11.30 a.m. I found Alice waiting with Miss Prickett at the station, and walked with them to Charlton Kings, about one and a half miles.

Carroll's presence was very welcome and he was prevailed upon to prolong his visit at Cheltenham and make further visits to Hetton Lawn. On the Monday it rained all day and the children were forced to remain in the schoolroom, but that was no hardship when Mr Dodgson was there to tell stories, play games and show them his latest photographs. In the evening, after a day cooped up, everybody went to the

Tenniel's illustration of Alice going through the mirror at her grandmother's 'Looking-Glass House' at Charlton Kings.

Assembly Rooms in Cheltenham to see the great magician, Herr Döbler (proclaimed by the local newspaper as 'the greatest wonder of the age') perform. His 'Enchanted Palace of Illusions' had been shown to Queen Victoria and one of his most popular feats was 'The Enchanted Garden' where it was said, 'He will plant on a common flowerpot a Rose and before you have time to think, behold the whole place is transformed to an Enchanted Garden and everyone will be supplied with fresh roses from the branches.'

As Carroll walked over to Hetton Lawn the next day for a final visit, there was much to fantasise about grandmother's magic mirror and her Garden of Live Flowers. When Carroll came to write *Through the Looking-Glass* Rhoda, although left behind in Oxford with their nurse, makes an appearance as the Rose, and the sister who was not born until the following year was given a tiny part as the Violet: when the Violet spoke in the flowerbed she naturally made Alice jump, 'for it hadn't spoken before'.

As we know from the writing of *Wonderland*, those present when the story was told appear as characters. Undoubtedly, Miss Prickett, who was with the Liddell children all the time the *Looking-Glass* adventures at Hetton Lawn and on the outings were being told, is the Red Queen. When Carroll was later asked to give instructions for a stage version of his books, many years after Miss Prickett had left the Liddells' service, he said that the Red Queen should be 'the concentrated essence of all governesses, formal and strict and pedantic but not unkind'. The children called her 'Pricks' and when the Red Queen first makes her appearance in the 'Garden of Live Flowers' in Looking-Glass House, Alice is told that, 'She's one of the thorny kind.' Certainly Tenniel manages to make the Red Queen look

The Red Queen, 'the quintessence of governesses', lectures Alice on Leckhampton Hill. By the time the second volume of *Alice* was published the fashion in socks had changed, as Tenniel duly notes: the heroine now has stripey socks.

rather fierce and spiky when she is wagging her finger at Alice on the breezy walk they took up the hill above Looking-Glass House. She is urging everyone on regardless of the wind that was 'whistling in Alice's ears, and almost blowing her hair off her head', but she shows her kind streak on this occasion by offering Alice dry biscuits when she is breathless after being run off her feet.

The Leckhampton episode is recorded in Carroll's diary:

> April 4. In the afternoon we went a large party in the carriage to Birdlip, where Ina, Alice and Miss Prickett got out, and walked back with me over Leckhampton Hill. Except for the high wind, the day could hardly have been better for the view: the children were in the wildest spirits.

From the escarpment, they had a wonderful view of the Gloucestershire plain in all directions, and talked about the geography of the area. Carroll pointed out the source of the River Thames at Seven Springs and promised to take them there if there was any time left during his stay. Alice warmed to this kind of geography and observed in *Through the Looking-Glass* that 'the first thing to do was to make a grand survey of the country . . . Principal mountains – I'm on the only one'. More fun, however, was when Carroll pretended to continue to play their fantasy game of chess on the square fields beneath Birdlip, which was recalled when he came to write *Through the Looking-Glass*:

> For some minutes Alice stood without speaking, looking out in all directions over the country – and a most curious country it was. There were a number of tiny little brooks running straight across it from side to side, and the ground between was divided up into squares by a number of little green hedges, that reached from brook to brook.

'I declare it's marked out just like a large chess-board!' Alice said at last. 'There ought to be some men moving about somewhere – and so there are!' she added in a tone of delight, and her heart began to beat with excitement as she went on. 'It's a great huge game of chess that's being played – all over the world – if this *is* the world at all, you know. Oh, what fun it is! How I *wish* I was one of them! I wouldn't mind being a Pawn, if only I might join – though of course I should *like* to be a Queen, best.'

When they got back to Hetton Lawn after their instructive and entertaining afternoon Carroll records that they 'found Mr. C. Liddell, who had arrived in our absence', and he would undoubtedly have had much more information to add about the 'most curious country' Alice had just been observing.

XII

Railways, Crests and Anglo-Saxons

Uncle Charles had just completed his own 'grand survey' of
the area: he was the engineer in charge of the proposed new
East Gloucestershire Railway. Charles Liddell had been
apprenticed to George Stephenson, Lewis Carroll's hero of
Croft railway days, whose first locomotive, the 'Rocket',
had been financed by Sir Henry Thomas Liddell, Alice's
grandfather's brother. All the Liddells had taken an interest
in railways in the north east and Charles Liddell built many
railways there before he became involved with surveying
the route for the one in East Gloucestershire.

The proposer of the scheme that would have brought a
station to Charlton Kings was the Hetton Lawn neighbour
and local MP, Sir William Russell of Charlton Park.
However, considerable opposition to the railway was voiced
by Cheltenham residents, who felt that the extension would
damage the setting of the Regency spa, and the project was
withdrawn. Sir William tried in vain to present a new accept-
able scheme but word was received at the end of March
1863, just when the Liddell children arrived at Hetton Lawn,
that the proposed East Gloucestershire Railway Company
must be wound up. It was then that Charles Liddell appeared
on the scene to take over the negotiations and was subsequently involved in two other attempts to get a railway
through Charlton Kings – these, too, ended in failure and it
was not until 1881 that the line was finally opened.

Alice's grandparents, who had moved to Charlton Kings in 1860, were heavily involved, as shareholders, in supporting their neighbour and their engineer son in the proposed railway. The news that the scheme had failed caused considerable anxiety amongst the investors and railway shares must have figured largely in the conversation at Hetton Lawn over the Easter holiday. Although all this was over Alice's head, 'The land there is worth a thousand pounds an inch' seemed about right. This was her remark in the Looking-Glass railway carriage, on the way home, when the guard accused her of not having a ticket, but then, as she said, ' "there wasn't a ticket-office where I came from" ' – having come from Charlton Kings, which had just learned that it would not have its own railway station after all.

The children had boarded the train at Cheltenham *en route* for Oxford and at Gloucester had been joined by Carroll, who had spent the previous week in Wales. His diary records:

> April 16th. The train from Cheltenham at 2.40 brought the three Liddells and Miss Prickett: we had a very merry journey to Oxford together.

Gloucester was a notoriously confusing station for an unwary traveller, for it was the junction of two different railways, one broad and one narrow gauge, and all those going north to Birmingham were required to change there. From Cheltenham to Swindon there was no need to change as the Oxford-bound travellers would be broad gauge all the way; the train from Cheltenham did, however, have to back out of the station on to the broad-gauge line, which was confusing to Alice, who now found herself travelling backwards.

Alice in a broad-gauge, first-class railway carriage returning to Oxford.
The train had had to turn round at Gloucester and Alice thought she was
'travelling the wrong way'.

All this time the Guard was looking at her, first through a
telescope, then through a microscope, then through an opera-
glass. At last he said, "You're travelling the wrong way," and
shut up the window, and went away.

The homeward-bound party travelled through the curious
checker-board countryside that had so interested Alice when
she surveyed it from the top of Leckhampton Hill and, as
Carroll always had a map in his black bag on railway
journeys, they could follow the route down the Stroud valley
and check the number of little brooks with the number of
wooden bridges they went over on the way to Swindon.
When the train crossed a brook it apparently jumped, which

made Alice a little nervous and 'in another moment she felt the carriage rise straight up into the air, and in her fright she caught at the thing nearest to her hand, which happened to be the Goat's beard'. At some stage the carriage also seems to have filled with insects of which Alice, of course, was never particularly fond. Seizing the Goat's beard was a correction suggested by Tenniel when he considered seriously the positioning of the strange passengers in the railway carriage he had to illustrate. An old lady, who would have got in the way, had to be removed from the text. Tenniel had with or without instructions made it a first-class broad-gauge railway carriage in which Lewis Carroll and the Liddell children had 'had a very merry journey to Oxford together' from Looking-Glass House.

The close relationship with the Liddell children, which had been strengthened by the Cheltenham holiday, continued after they returned to Oxford. Games (he invented a new one called 'Croquet Castles' for them), walks round Oxford, learning to feather their oars on the river and story-telling were constantly demanded. A new pastime they had begun in the winter was crest-collecting, then very fashionable with young ladies. A large number of the letters received at the Deanery from family, friends and old members of Christ Church bore crests, which the children cut out and arranged in artistic patterns. Lewis Carroll had been asked to help the children with their crest books and when they returned home after three weeks' absence there would have been an accumulation of letterheads and envelopes to deal with.

Learning about heraldry with Lewis Carroll would have provided great scope for imaginative story-telling. The Liddell's own crest was, of course, the first one to explore:

it was a black lion rampant crowned with an Eastern crown of gold, very like the one Alice would wear later when she became Queen. The Liddell coat of arms sported three leopards' faces, grinning like Cheshire cats, and, for supporters, two more splendid leopards with crowns round their necks or, as it said in the language of heraldry, 'gorged with mural crowns purp'. Alice learned that supporters were needed to stand either side of the shields of important families. At the end of *Through the Looking-Glass*, when Alice is required to give a speech, she is reminded by the White Queen that both she and her Red counterpart must support her when she stands up.

Alice, of course, had had two real, rather than heraldic, 'supporters' during the business of growing up: her governess, known to be the Red Queen, and her old nurse, Phoebe Hall, who seems effortlessly to fit the part of the White Queen, whose hair was always coming down and her shawl falling off. The White Queen was very caring and maternal and the first words she utters at the beginning of *Looking-Glass*, as she tries to find the little pawn that has fallen into the hearth, are, ' "It is the voice of my child! . . . My precious Lily!" ' The Red Queen, clearly the superior piece, took care of the children's general education and behaviour and accompanied them on their outings. The good-natured but down-trodden White Queen was concerned with such things as 'a-dressing' the children, brushing and combing hair, applying plasters and seeing that enough bread and butter was eaten before they got jam tomorrow.

The White Queen was very easily frightened (as was the nurse) for we are told at the beginning of *Through the Looking-Glass* that once Alice 'had really frightened her old nurse by shouting suddenly in her ear, "Nurse! Do let's

pretend that I'm a hungry hyaena, and you're a bone!" ' The
White Queen was particularly frightened of storms and when
she began to say, ' "It was *such* a thunderstorm, you can't
think!" ' the Red Queen told Alice on the side, ' "She *never*
could, you know" ' but she admitted that she was 'a dear
good creature' if you treated her kindly. The White Queen
was also apparently a keen knitter: when she becomes transformed into the Sheep in the shop (in 'Wool and Water'), she
could work fourteen pairs of knitting needles at once. Alice's
shop, where her nurse took her to buy her favourite barley
sugar and which is duly illustrated by Tenniel, still exists in St
Aldate's, opposite Christ Church.

Carroll was so busy with the children's requirements that
the only entry he made in his diary for over a week was:

Tenniel's illustration for 'He's an Anglo-Saxon messenger and those are
Anglo-Saxon attitudes'.

No hpaðne celmihtig. túlna polde. adame geuan
anna oftion. pæðth ætpynnde. þiih þe he him pnom
rpice. ác he him topropne. læthpaðene pond pçan
hynredne hnop. halgum tunglum. Thim gund pe
lan ginne rtalde. het þam rin hipum. per Tibidian
tuddor tbnona na. táblha gehilene. toponuld nytte.
perrmar pædan. Geraton þa ætrti rynne. rorgrul
ne land. tario Tedyl. unrpedignan. þnemðna gehpilene.
þonne rerpum rtol per. þehie arcah oede. or aðþu
çth pundon. Ongunnon hie þa begoðt hærre. bæpun
arduhan. Trah him meod bebiað. adamir Teuan
aronan pærnon. Enfolicu tpa rnum bænn clined.
cam Tabel ut cyðað bec. huþa ðæd rruman dyge
þartrynydon. pelan Trirte pill gebnoðon.

The Caedmon Genesis *c.* 1000, which was exhibited at
the Bodleian Library in 1863.

> 29 April. There is no variety in my life to record just now except meetings with the Liddells, the record of which has become almost continuous.

A new place for the children to visit was the Bodleian Library, whose treasures were hitherto only available to scholars who could locate them in the catalogue. Henry Coxe, appointed Bodley's Librarian in 1860, was a close friend of Dean Liddell, himself a Curator of the Bodleian. Together they promoted the idea of having a small public exhibition area which would, Coxe noted in his diary, bring 'to life things hidden away and forgotten'. In the spring of 1863 they put on an exhibition to show the progress of the arts of calligraphy and illumination in England which included the famous Anglo-Saxon Caedmon manuscripts. Tenniel's illustration of Haigha, the Anglo-Saxon messenger with his cross gartering and shoon and his ham sandwich bag, is straight out of the Caedmon Genesis. Alice is seen to be much amused by his extraordinary out-turned hands and feet, although she would have been too well behaved to laugh outright and would certainly have waited until she got outside the Bodleian precincts before trying out 'Anglo-Saxon attitudes' herself.

XIII

The Royal Visit to Oxford

In May 1863, Oxford's plans for the visit of the royal couple had reached fever pitch. The last official Royal Visit had been by the Prince Regent in 1814, although there had been private visits such as Queen Victoria's sudden appearance when the Prince of Wales was an undergraduate. The happy pair were to stay three days at the Deanery where elaborate preparations were being made. The new Liddell baby's christening was postponed so that the Prince, who had chosen the names Albert Edward, could stand as godfather but, sadly, the baby died at the end of May. Carroll did everything he could to get the children out of the house at such a distressing time for the family.

One of the chief civic events was to be the Bazaar in St John's garden in aid of funds for the Radcliffe Infirmary at which all the leading ladies of the county, including Mrs Liddell, had agreed to hold stalls. The day before the royal arrival on 16 June, Lewis Carroll was taken over to the Deanery to see the articles for the Bazaar and had a preview of the splendidly furnished chamber and royal bedstead, which he was later allowed to photograph, with Alice and her sister sitting importantly on the window seat behind it.

The great day dawned. Oxford was bedecked with flags and flowers and bells rang out all over the city. At a quarter to one the great gates of Christ Church opened and the royal procession entered Tom Quad. Under an awning stood the

Dean and Mrs Liddell and beside them on the red carpet their excited children, with Alice, like her namesake, frantically trying to remember the Red Queen's instructions about curtseying and behaving in royal presences (' "Curtsey while you're thinking what to say" ' and ' "Look up, speak nicely, and don't twiddle your fingers all the time" '). It rained incessantly and the Dean was in constant attendance on the Princess with an umbrella, while she presented prizes to the University Volunteers drawn up in the quad. The brass band seemed to be in difficulties, although, according to *Punch* (and did Carroll sometimes send contributions himself?), the Dean of Christ Church had made provisions for the star *cornet-à-piston* performer to do so 'under a horning' in inclement weather. Lewis Carroll watched the proceedings, out of the rain, with a telescope from a window in a room overlooking Tom Quad, his friend having obligingly removed a pane of glass to make it easier for him.

Then followed three days of non-stop festivities in Oxford: the Prince's honorary degree at the Sheldonian, the Bazaar, the *Encaenia* (the annual Commemoration of the University's founders), a masonic fête, the Deanery garden party, two balls, a procession of boats and the Grand Banquet at Christ Church. The Liddell children, including four-year-old Rhoda, took part in many of the events and were particularly concerned to help their mother at the Bazaar. Lewis Carroll records this in some detail and the incident of the Liddell kittens is particularly relevant to Alice's *Looking-Glass* adventures, since kittens figure prominently in the second volume of *Alice*.

I had intended to go only into the gardens and not into the Bazaar itself, but when I got there the Bazaar was not yet open, so I thought I would go and make myself useful to the

78

The royal visit was a memorable occasion for Alice. The picture shows the presentation of prizes to the University Volunteers, in pouring rain, by Princess Alexandra on 16 June 1863.

Liddells. After I had helped in their stall for a short time, the Royal party arrived; there were very few admitted with them and the place was comparatively clear; I crept under the counter and joined the children outside, and the Prince (I don't know whether he knew me) bowed and made a remark about a picture. The children were selling some white kittens (like Persian) and as Alice dared not offer hers to the Princess, I volunteered to plead further, and asked the Prince if the Princess would not like a kitten – on which she turned and said to me; 'Oh, but I've bought one of those kittens already' (which I record is the only remark she is ever likely to make to me). Ina's had already been the favoured one. For some time I went about with the children, trying to get their kittens sold, when suddenly the Bazaar was opened, and the place filled with a dense mob. Rhoda was missing, and I set out to hunt her up, with Edith, who insisted on coming too, and after some time I spied her out in a stall: I begged them to hand her over to me, and carrying her and pushing Edith, I fought my way down the whole Bazaar through a tremendous crush, back to the stall.

The next day, while the royals were being entertained elsewhere, Lewis Carroll and the Liddell children went back to the Bazaar at St John's, but Alice was very anxious about the time as, in spite of their heavy engagements, the Prince and Princess had asked for time to be set aside for them to play croquet with the Deanery children, and Carroll noted in his diary that, on schedule, 'the children left at 4 to play croquet with the royal guests'. Clearly Alice had made much of this, hence the playful solemnity of the illustration for 'invitation from the Queen to play croquet' in the 'Pig and Pepper' chapter of *Wonderland*: this was part of the material, additional to the manuscript *Under Ground*, which was inserted after the decision to publish was taken in 1863.

Alice had been promised, in her fantasy game of chess in *Through the Looking-Glass*, that when she reached the eighth square she would become a queen herself and from then on it would be 'all feasting and fun'. When Alice was told that she would be required to give a royal dinner party, however, she became concerned about invitations and was very relieved on reaching the hall to find that everyone was already there; ' "I'm glad they've come without waiting to be asked," she thought: "I should never have known who were the right people to invite!" ' This was a matter which had exercised the Deanery for weeks before the real Christ Church royal banquet. A galaxy of dukes and duchesses, prelates, professors and statesmen (including Gladstone and Disraeli) had accepted and the arrangements were reported to be 'extensive and magnificent in the extreme and the banquet on a most gorgeous scale'. The Great Hall had been redecorated and newly lit with gas. The menu included the usual 'beautiful soup', 'Salmon, come up' and the Leg of Mutton, which unlike the one at Alice's banquet, certainly was cut up. The Dean and Mrs Liddell sat at High Table with their royal guests under the portrait of the royal Founder, Henry VIII, and Lewis Carroll sat in the body of the Hall and recorded that it was 'a day to be remembered as unique and most interesting', although he found the music during the banquet much too loud for his liking.

Alice's mock banquet was very like the real thing with introductions, protocol, toasts and waiting on royal words. Alice found this aspect a little frightening when as a royal person 'the moment she opened her lips, there was dead silence, and all eyes were fixed upon her'. She was also afraid that her crown might come off. The last illustration showing the Banquet brings together the royal theme which

The Royal Banquet, which ends the game of Alice's royal make-believe.
The Christ Church ceremonial plate is falling off High Table, but the
port decanters have acquired wings.

runs right through the *Looking-Glass* story. The fireworks which were anticipated in the first chapter take off from the silver candlesticks when, finally, as the dream comes to an end, Alice pulls the tablecloth off High Table, knocking the ceremonial plate and the dessert on the floor. (Was it Carroll or Tenniel who saved the port by making the decanters acquire wings and take off – presumably for the Common Room?) For Alice it was the grand climax to the game of royal make-believe, and now that she had become a queen herself she would have to say goodbye to her don friend and leave behind her adventures in Wonderland and the Looking-Glass world.

XIV

Nuneham and the White Knight's Farewell

The Harcourts' Thamesside landscaped park at Nuneham had a special significance for Carroll as it was here, at the end of the 1863 summer term, he said goodbye to Alice's childhood friendship, although at the time he did not know that this was to be their last excursion together. He had already accepted that Ina would not be allowed to join in when the time for river trips came round again the next spring, but he recorded in his diary for 1864:

> May 12, (Th) During these last few days I have applied in vain for leave to take the children on the river, i.e. Alice, Edith and Rhoda: but Mrs Liddell will not let any come in future – rather superfluous caution.

When Carroll came to assemble his material for *Through the Looking-Glass*, checking it with his diary, he realised that the last precious excursion was that to Nuneham in June 1863. ' "I'll see you safe to the end of the wood – and then I must go back, you know. That's the end of my move," ' said Alice's White Knight.

Nuneham had always been a favourite full-day river excursion, which the eighty-year-old Alice remembered with special pleasure in her 'Recollections':

Nuneham Park, the scene of many a happy picnic, showing the cottages described by Alice. The last outing she had with Carroll was to Nuneham.

On rarer occasions we went out for the whole day with him, and then we took a larger basket with luncheon – cold chicken, and salad, and all sorts of good things. One of our favourite whole day excursions was to row down to Nuneham and picnic in the woods there, in one of the huts specially provided by Mr Harcourt for picnickers. On landing at Nuneham, our first duty was to choose the hut, and then to borrow plates, glasses, knives and forks from the cottages by the riverside. To us the hut might have been a Fairy King's palace, and the picnic a banquet in our honour. Sometimes we were told stories after luncheon that transported us into Fairyland. Sometimes we spent the afternoon wandering in the more material fairyland of the Nuneham woods until it was time to row back to Oxford in the long summer evening.

The early trips to Nuneham were made on the special days, Tuesdays and Thursdays, when the owner of Nuneham, William Harcourt, allowed river visitors to land and picnic in the huts he provided in the woods, as Alice described. Later, however, when William Harcourt's nephew, Augustus Vernon Harcourt, became a college friend and subsequently an oarsman on some of the river trips, Carroll's party was able to walk through the part of the landscaped park which was out of bounds to other visitors. Vernon Harcourt, who first became associated with Christ Church in 1860, was Lee's Reader in Chemistry and made the college laboratory, converted from the old Anatomy School, into an outstanding centre for his subject. His first recorded river trip with Carroll was a month after the famous outing to Godstow on 4 July 1862, when *Alice's Adventures Under Ground* were told. Whether or not Carroll intended that this was the end of the adventures, the children thought otherwise and he records in his diary that the suggestion of playing games was turned down and he was forced to continue 'the interminable fairy-tale of Alice's Adventures' on this vacation trip when Harcourt was fellow oarsman.

Duckworth, as we know, had been the Duck, and Wilfred the Gryphon, when oarsmen in the *Under Ground* story-telling excursions, Miss Prickett had been given the Red Queen's part at Hetton Lawn, so a character must surely be found for Harcourt in the continued adventures, which were later to appear in *Looking-Glass*. He was given manuscript pages of *Looking-Glass* to read before publication, and his children in later years saw the White Knight's inventive and absent-minded eccentricities, such as the upside-down sandwich box and the mouse-trap and the bee-hive, which he carried on his horse in case of eventualities, as inspired by those of their father. Certainly the case that Christine King makes out for Harcourt as 'Chemistry's White Knight' (in her article in *New Scientist*, 28 June 1979) is an intriguing one. Augustus Vernon Harcourt's speciality, which earned him an FRS in 1863 was chemical reactions (' "You've no idea what a difference it makes, mixing it with other things – such as gunpowder and sealing-wax," ' said the experimentalist White Knight) and his original contribution to the *course* of chemical change was the time factor which had not been previously appreciated (' "a very clever pudding to invent" ' in between courses).

Carroll was also, like the White Knight, 'a great hand at inventing things' as anyone who saw the room he finally moved into on the St Aldate's front at Christ Church in 1868 could testify. Christopher Hussey, who occupied it in 1925, spoke of the family of thermometers and how,

Tenniel's illustration of the White Knight. Carroll saw himself as the knight escorting Alice until she grew out of childhood.

"I'll see you safe to the end of the wood – and then I must go back, you know. That's the end of my move."

whenever one fell or rose from the mean, an adjacent stove had to be adjusted to rectify the variation, and an ingenious gas chandelier, that only the author of *Alice* could light, even after reading the instructions that covered the door. Carroll was, Hussey said, 'an embodiment of the White Knight, full of his own inventions'. Carroll inventions included a nyctograph for note-taking in the dark and tiny liqueur scales for fair measure in the Senior Common Room. He certainly felt, like the White Knight, that 'it's as well to be provided for *everything*' (when he visited the seaside he carried large safety pins in his black bag to offer to any nanny whose charge might be prevented from paddling for fear of getting her frock wet).

There is no doubt that when Carroll came to write down *Looking-Glass* he wanted the actual character of the White Knight, the piece in the chess game that would escort Alice to the end of the game, for himself. He gave explicit instructions to Tenniel not to give him whiskers and not to make him look old, which the illustrator obviously disregarded, and indeed the White Knight has a look of Tenniel himself. Carroll seems to have taken the image of the Knight escorting the child from the painting 'Sir Isumbras at the Ford' by Millais (whom Carroll had met and greatly admired) and it is how he wanted Alice to remember him.

> Of all the strange things that Alice saw in her journey Through the Looking-Glass, this was the one that she always remembered most clearly. Years afterwards she could bring the whole scene back again, as if it had been only yesterday – the mild blue eyes and kindly smile of the Knight – the setting sun gleaming through his hair, and shining on his armour in a blaze of light . . . all this she took in like a picture.

Perhaps a solution to the Harcourt/White Knight tradition might be that, as in the chess game, there were meant to be two knights. The real White Knight does refer to 'the other White Knight' who once got into his helmet by mistake and, furthermore, when the White King sends all his horses to rescue Humpty Dumpty he insists that two should be kept back 'because two of them are wanted in the game'. All the king's horses were very much part of the fantasy of the last trip to Nuneham on 25 June 1863. On the Thursday, Carroll accompanied Miss Prickett and the children to Sanger's Circus and Monster Hippodrome, where they saw a procession of bareback-ridden horses half a mile long and equestrian exercises said to be 'on a scale never before attempted in the world'. The next day was the Grand Volunteer review with 8000 cavalry and infantry engaging in a Sham Fight before 50,000 people in Port Meadow. Drums and cannons thundered all day and a pall of smoke hung over the city. There was great crowding and confusion when it all ended promptly at six and everyone tried to leave together. The Volunteers in their Sham Fight, like Tweedledum and Tweedledee, had fought till six and then had dinner. Carroll's diary reads:

> 24 June. Great Volunteer review in Port Meadow . . . there I
> fell in with the Liddells and with Hoole: we waited
> to see them safe off.

Soldiers, drums and horses were much in the children's minds when they played make-believe in Nuneham woods the next day. The White King asks Alice, ' "Did you happen to meet any soldiers, my dear, as you came through the wood?" "Yes, I did," says Alice: "several thousand, I should think." '

Vernon Harcourt must have warned his relations about this especially large four-oar river trip to Nuneham, which included, besides himself and Carroll, the Dean and his wife, the four girls and their grandfather. They all had tea under the trees and when the rest of the party were met by a carriage and driven back, Carroll walked on with Ina, Edith, and Alice to go back by train. It was, indeed, *mirabile dictu*, as Carroll recorded in his diary, that he and the children could be on their own as they walked through Lock Wood to Culham station. There would have been little chance to fantasise during the day but this was just the opportunity they needed, with no other grown-up present, to turn the unforgettable events of the previous week into Alice's adventures. 'A pleasant expedition with a *very* pleasant conclusion,' wrote Carroll. When he came to write *Through the Looking-Glass* he realised that this Nuneham event was the last real meeting with Alice; thereafter there were only casual encounters. The magic and rapport had gone. The White Knight's retrospective farewell is, therefore, particularly poignant.

' "You've only a few yards to go," he said, "down the hill and over that little brook, and then you'll be a Queen – But you'll stay and see me off first?" he added as Alice turned away with an eager look in the direction to which he pointed. "I shan't be long. You'll wait and wave your handkerchief when I get to that turn in the road? I think it'll encourage me, you see." '

XV

'So you're another Alice'

The final full title for the second volume of Alice, published in 1872, was *Through the Looking-Glass, and what Alice found there*. It was apparently little Alice Raikes who gave Carroll the idea of sending the heroine through the looking-glass, rather than relating the episodes to *Alice's Visit to Looking-Glass House*, which was the original title. Meeting her in his uncle's house at Onslow Square in London, he said, 'So you're another Alice. I'm very fond of Alices.' They were standing in front of a long mirror and, giving her an orange in her right hand, he asked her in which hand the little girl in the mirror held it, and she replied, 'The left hand . . . but if I was on the other side of the glass, wouldn't the orange still be in my right?' He was very pleased with the answer and said that it had given him an idea for *Through the Looking-Glass*, an early copy of which the little girl was sent. *Behind the Looking-Glass* was first thought of as the new title but Carroll's close friend and colleague, Dr Harry Liddon, preferred *Through the Looking-Glass*. Liddon, who was notorious for nursing the common-room cat upside down, may already have had a tribute in *Wonderland*, when Alice is nursing the pig baby in this fashion.

Through the Looking-Glass also contains episodes harking back to Carroll's northern background, not directly related to Alice's own adventures, as it was still being written several years after the Alice story-telling had ceased. Carroll spent part of the Christmas vacation of 1867 visiting his Wilcox cousins in Whitburn, where twelve years before he had composed the 'Jabberwocky' poem, which first appeared in *Mischmasch* as a 'Stanza of Anglo-Saxon poetry'. Carroll's nephew, Stuart Dodgson Collingwood, said that, in 1855, 'to while away an evening, the whole party sat down to a game of verse-making and "Jabberwocky" was his contribution'. The 'Jabberwocky', with its world famous 'Twas Brillig and the slithy toves, did gyre and gimble in the wabe' lines, comes from a Beowulf background, where dragons are called worms. Carroll was very familiar with such north-country legends, particularly as a ceremony took place on the bridge at Croft, which was a reminder of the slaying of the Sockburn worm which had terrorised the district in pre-Conquest times. Nearer to Whitburn were the equally famous legendary monsters, the Lambton Worm and the Laidley Worm.

Carroll always called on Tom Harrison, the chief engineer of the North Eastern Railway, when visiting Whitburn. Writing in *Country Life* on 3 May 1973, his granddaughter recalled that her mother had said that the children 'looked forward to Mr Dodgson's visits, as he took them for walks on the sands telling them all about *Through the Looking-Glass*'. If these stories were special to the Harrison children walking on the Whitburn sands, then it would be a seaside story he told, and that must surely be 'The Walrus and the Carpenter', which, unlike 'Jabberwocky', had not appeared in family magazines before. There were certainly 'quantities of sand' along the beach between Whitburn and Seaburn, and the Harrison family was connected with shipbuilding and ships' carpenters in nearby Sunderland and, for full measure, their uncle Dick, who came to them for holidays, was a famous arctic explorer who knew all about walruses. Sunderland has its own stuffed walrus in the museum and likes to claim that that, and Tenniel's distinctive box-like headdress worn by the Sunderland ships' carpenters, proves the location of 'The Walrus and the Carpenter'.

There were many more child friendships to make in Oxford in the 1880s, after the university reforms abolished the celibacy rule for college fellowships. Married dons were required to set up home within a mile of Carfax, the centre of Oxford. As their numerous Alices, Mauds, Enids and Beatrices grew into children, Carroll, who himself preferred not to forsake the Christ Church Common Room for the permanent matrimonial delights of the North Oxford suburb, was constantly called in to entertain with readings of his 'Bruno's Picnic' or 'The Hunting of the Snark'. Games that he had invented (Lanrick, Syzygies, Symbolic Logic problems and Croquet Castles) were played in many dons' homes and Mad Hatters' tea-parties performed for his benefit. His Puzzles, *Wonderland* postage-stamp cases and biscuit tins were handed out and, of course, *Alice* books, signed in violet ink 'from the author'. He 'borrowed' the North Oxford children for walks in the University Parks and for his special Oxford tours, and he had them to tea in his rooms, which he kept full of toys and games. At one time there was a list of 107 names of little girls to be photographed grouped under Christian names with birthdays.

'Don't children ever bore you?' asked an incredulous undergraduate. 'Little children are three-fourths of my life, I don't see how they could bore anyone,' was the bachelor don's sincere reply.

Carroll still saw himself in the role of the White Knight: indeed one nine man's morris game he had made was inscribed 'To Olive from the White Knight'. Olive Butler later told her niece that they all knew he was the White Knight as he spoke just like him. He wrote hundreds of delightful letters to children, like miniature Wonderlands, which have now been published, but one little girl who had scarlet fever and received a new puzzle or cypher letter every day for six weeks, bitterly resented that hers were burned for fear of harbouring germs. Many of the later child friends were those he met on seaside holidays, or child actresses, particularly those who played in the stage productions of *Alice*. In the late 1880s Carroll went on to teach Symbolic Logic to older girls at the Oxford High School and the women's colleges, which he felt would train them to think independently and analytically to safeguard them from false statements made by politicians and what we now call the media.

The *Alice* books were never far from Carroll's mind. Each new edition was carefully checked and in 1878 he reprimanded Macmillan for the disappearance of both kings from the chess diagram at the beginning of *Looking-Glass* in a copy of the forty-second-thousand printing. There were French and German translations in 1869, an Italian in 1872 and an abridged Dutch edition in 1874, which gave him the idea of a shortened *Nursery Alice* with colour pictures for children 'from nought to five', which was finally published in 1889. In 1885 Carroll wrote to Alice, then Mrs Hargreaves, living at Lyndhurst, to seek her permission to publish a facsimile of the manuscript *Under Ground* in her possession. 'I have had scores of child friends since your time,' he wrote, 'but they have been quite a different thing.'

95

The Duck was one of the first to receive a copy of the facsimile, published in 1886, inscribed 'The Duck from the Dodo'. Alice's special copy, bound in white vellum, said it all, forty years on, 'To Her whose namesake one happy summer day inspired this story.'

Carroll died in Guildford on 14 January 1898, while spending the Christmas holiday with his sisters. His obituary tributes included scores from former child friends, one of whom helped to set up a fund for an *Alice in Wonderland* memorial cot at Great Ormond Street Hospital for Sick Children. For the 1932 Centenary of his birth, a fund was also set up for a Lewis Carroll children's ward at St Mary's Hospital, Paddington, where his nephew, Bertram Collingwood, was Professor of Physiology. In 1932, at the age of eighty, Alice Hargreaves crossed the Atlantic to be present at the Lewis Carroll Centenary Celebrations at Columbia University which were delayed to take place on her birthday, 4 May. When she was awarded an honorary degree for having inspired two great literary works she replied, 'I feel that Mr Dodgson knows and rejoices with me in the honour that you are doing him.' She afterwards told a reporter that to the most retiring of parsons the ceremony would have seemed as strange as the whimsical stories he used to tell her. 'I wonder how many stories the world has missed,' she added, 'because he never wrote anything down until I teased him into doing it.'

Alice's original manuscript of *Under Ground* was sold to a collector in the United States, but when it came on the market again in 1948, it was bought for $50,000 by a group of American well-wishers and returned to Great Britain as 'an expression of thanks to a noble people who had held Hitler at bay for a long period single-handed'. It was put on permanent display at the British Museum, where it was received by the Archbishop of Canterbury, who called the American gesture of generosity and friendship an 'unsullied and innocent act in a distracted and sinful world'. Carroll had published his nonsense stories, 'not for money, and not for fame, but in the hope of supplying, for the children whom I love, some thoughts that may suit those hours of innocent merriment which are the very life of Childhood: and also, in the hope of suggesting to them and to others, some thoughts that may prove, I would fain hope, not wholly out of harmony with the graver cadences of Life.'

The last page of the original manuscript of *Alice's Adventures Under Ground*. Carroll was apparently not satisfied with his drawing of the real Alice at the end of the book and pasted one of his photographs of her, aged seven, over it.

Select Book List

The Complete Works of Lewis Carroll, Nonesuch Press, 1939

Cohen, Morton (ed.), *The Letters of Lewis Carroll*, 2 vols,
    Macmillan, 1979
    ——*Lewis Carroll: Interviews and Recollections*, Macmillan,
    1989
    ——and Anita Gandolfo, *Lewis Carroll and the House of
    Macmillan*, Cambridge University Press, 1987

Collingwood, Stuart Dodgson, *The Life and Letters of Lewis
    Carroll*, Fisher Unwin, 1898

Fulford, R. (ed.), *Dearest Child*, Evans, 1964

Green, Roger Lancelyn (ed.), *The Diaries of Lewis Carroll*,
    Cassell, 1953
    ——*The Works of Lewis Carroll*, Paul Hamlyn, 1965 (includes
    a number of pieces omitted from the Nonesuch edition)

Hargreaves, Alice, 'Alice's Recollections of Carrollian Days', told
    to her son Caryl Hargreaves, *The Cornhill Magazine*, July
    1932

Thompson, H. L., *Memoir of Henry George Liddell*, 1899

William, S. H., F. Madan and R. L. Green, *The Lewis Carroll
    Handbook*, Oxford University Press, 1931 (revised edition
    Dawson, 1979)

SELECT BOOK LIST

*Macmillan's current editions which include
all Lewis Carroll's corrections to the text*

Alice's Adventures in Wonderland (New Children's Edition),
       Macmillan, 1980 (with eight plates in colour)
Through the Looking-Glass, and what Alice found there,
       Macmillan, 1980 (with eight plates in colour. The deleted
       chapter, 'The Wasp in a Wig', is included in an appendix)

Index

INDEX

Victoria, 23; walks with the Liddell children, 30, 33; river excursions, 36, 43; expedition to Nuneham, 37–8, 40; attitude to University politics, 41; tells 'Alice's Adventures Under Ground', 44, 46; asked by Alice to write down stories, 46–7; illustrations, 48, 49, 51–2, 54, 57; persuaded to publish, 48, 49; interest in art, 50–1; and John Tenniel, 52, 57–8; enjoys *Punch*, 54; tells *Through the Looking-Glass*, 57, 58; royal wedding, 58–60, 61; royal visit to Christ Church, 77–8, 79–81; visits Hetton Lawn, 63; visit to Leckhampton Hill, 67, 71; last real meeting with Alice, 91; publishes *Through the Looking-Glass*, 92–4; child friends after Alice, 94, 95; attitude to children, 94; editions of *Alice*, 95; death, 96

Dodgson, the Reverend Charles (father), 5, 8, 33
Dodgson, Edwin (brother), 5, 59
Dodgson, Elizabeth (sister), 5, 37
Dodgson, Frances (sister), 5, 37, 40
Dodgson, Frances Jane (mother), 5, 8
Dodgson, Henrietta (sister), 5
Dodgson, Louisa (sister), 5, 8
Dodgson, Mary (sister), 5
Dodgson, Menella (niece), 14
Dodgson Railway Game, 5–7
Dodgson, Skeffington (brother), 5, 12, 15, 20
Dodgson, Wilfred (brother), 5, 8, 12, 13, 14–15, 87
Dodo, the, 34–5, *39*, 40–2

Dormouse, the, 32
Duck, the, 40–1
Duckworth, the Reverend Robinson ('The Duck'), 12, 37, 38, 40, 43, 45, 46, 87, 96

Eaglet, the, 40–1
Edward, Prince of Wales (later Edward VII), 17–20, 23, 24–5, 34, 58, 59–60, 77–8, 80–1, 83
Election to the Hebdomadal Council, The, 41
Elementary Treatise of Determinants, An, 9

Father William, *46*
Fowler, Thomas, 11–12
Frewin Hall, 17, 25
Frikell, Wijaba, 20

Godstow, 12, 14, 38, 44–7, 57, 86
Grand Volunteer Review, 90
Great Exhibition, 25
Great Ormond Street Hospital, 96
Gryphon, the, 11, 12, *13*, 14–15, 87
Guildford, 8, 96

Hall, Phoebe, 73
Harcourt, Augustus Vernon, 86–7, 90
Harcourt, William, 86
Hargreaves, Alice *see* Liddell, Alice
Harrison, Tom, 93
Hetton Lawn, 63, 64, 70
'How doth the little busy bee', 19
Hughes, Arthur, 51
Humpty Dumpty, 7, 34, 90
Hussey Christopher, 87, 89
Huxley, Thomas, 35

Iffley, 37

INDEX